Gifts *from* the *Heart*

Food Gifts For All Occasions

Especially For You

Credits

Great American Opportunities, Inc./Favorite Recipes Press

President: Thomas F. McDow III

Editorial Manager: Mary Jane Blount
Editors: Georgia Brazil, Mary Cummings,
Jane Hinshaw, Linda Jones, Mary Wilson
Typography: Pam Newsome, Sara Anglin

Home Economics Advisory Board

Favorite Recipes Press wants to recognize the following persons
who graciously serve on our Home Economics Advisory Board:

Carolyn Cotton
Home Economics Teacher
Bristow, Oklahoma

Alma L. Payne
Home Economics Teacher
Hurst, Texas

Regina M. Haynes
Home Economics Teacher
Waynesville, North Carolina

Susan Rogers
Home Economics Teacher
Palos Verdes Estates, California

Brenda D. Long
Home Economics Teacher
Richlands, Virginia

Sue Shackelford
Home Economics Teacher
Hackleburg, Alabama

Emily Oates, State Supervisor
Home Economics Education
Little Rock, Arkansas

Sherry Zeigler
Home Economics Teacher
Chillicothe, Ohio

Cover Photograph: Hershey Foods Corporation

Copyright© 1989 by:
Great American Opportunities, Inc.
P.O. Box 305142
Nashville, TN 37230
Library of Congress Catalog Number: 89-1465
ISBN: 0-87197-250-6
Manufactured in the United States of America
First Printing 1989

Table of Contents

♥ *Introduction* ♥

Throughout history, food has always been a focal point for any important milestone, social gathering or celebration. There are few gifts that gladden the heart and warm the soul as do gifts from the kitchen.

This book is filled with wonderful recipes for a wide variety of very special foods for any gift occasion. As the saying goes, "Nothing says lovin' like something from the oven."

You know you can rely on every recipe to be the best, because they are tried and true favorites of home economics teachers all over America.

As publishers of Home Economics Cookbooks for over twenty-five years, Great American is proud to support home economics education.

Home economics is the only course that specifically prepares young men and women for the successful management of careers, homes and families.

Today's home economics curriculum includes important life skills such as:
- Home, Family and Resource Management
- Child Care and Development
- Individuals and Families in Crisis
- Consumer Education
- Substance Abuse
- AIDS and Other Diseases
- Teen Pregnancy
- Nutrition and Healthy Living

Help protect our nation's strength, our families. Please give your support to home economics education.

Tom McDow

Thomas F. McDow III
President

Gifts for All Occasions

♥ *Gifts of Love* ♥

Whether we're trying to say "happy anniversary" or "bon voyage," a gift of lovingly prepared food tells the recipients that they're someone special to us. When we bring that Mom's-recipe coconut cake to a christening party, or send the next door neighbor a batch of his favorite fudge in honor of a promotion, we're conveying a message that's just as cherished as the goodies it accompanies.

Gifts from the kitchen don't always have to be elaborate presentations to get that message across. Here, you'll find wonderful, hearty recipes for gift breads that are a real treat in this age of cellophane-wrapped supermarket loaves. On the other hand, you undoubtedly won't want to miss our heavenly, and only slightly more complex, cake recipes when you're planning such red-letter calendar events as Valentine's Day or that special birthday.

Our section on gift candies will erase any lingering doubts you might harbor about tackling the confectioner's art. The only truly difficult part of these recipes is resisting too much sampling of the finished product!

You'll also find fresh ideas about that most-given food gift of all: cookies. They go to camp, college and the army. They visit hospitals and churches. They look elegant at weddings and down-home picnics. In all their forms, from humble sugar cookies to sophisticated, lacy creations, nothing conjures up memories of cozy kitchens and warm hearts so well.

Finally there are dozens of special jams, relishes and mixes of all kinds which you can make ahead when time and ingredients are plentiful and keep on hand for instant gifts.

In today's fast-paced, high-tech world, when so few of us have the time, homemade gifts for any occasion–holidays or special days–from the kitchen are all the more special, showing that you care enough to give a little bit of yourself.

♥ *Bread Gifts* ♥

Apple Butter Bread

1/2 cup butter or margarine,
   softened
1 cup packed light brown sugar
1 egg
2 cups all-purpose flour
2 teaspoons cinnamon
2 teaspoons nutmeg

2 teaspoons allspice
1 teaspoon cloves
2 teaspoons soda
3/4 cup buttermilk
1 cup apple butter
1/2 cup chopped pecans

Preheat oven to 350 degrees. Cream butter and brown sugar in mixer bowl until light and fluffy. Blend in egg. Combine flour and spices in bowl. Mix soda and buttermilk in cup. Add dry ingredients to creamed mixture alternately with buttermilk mixture, mixing well after each addition. Stir in apple butter and pecans. Pour into greased 5x9-inch loaf pan. Bake for 40 minutes. Reduce temperature to 325 degrees. Bake for 20 minutes or until loaf tests done. Cool in pan for 5 minutes. Invert onto serving plate. Yield: 1 loaf.

Jackie Fuqua, Florida

Cranberry and Cheese Bread

1 1/2 cups chopped cranberries
1/2 cup sugar
2 cups all-purpose flour
1 tablespoon baking powder
1/2 teaspoon salt
3/4 cup sugar
1 cup chopped pecans

1 1/2 cups shredded Cheddar
   cheese
1 egg, slightly beaten
1 cup milk
1/2 cup melted butter or
   margarine

Preheat oven to 350 degrees. Mix cranberries with 1/2 cup sugar in bowl. Chill in refrigerator. Sift flour, baking powder, salt and remaining 3/4 cup sugar into bowl. Add pecans, cheese and cranberries. Add egg, milk and butter; mix gently. Pour into greased 5x9-inch loaf pan. Bake for 1 hour. Yield: 1 loaf.

Missy Markham, Arkansas

Avocado Bread

2²/3 cups sifted all-purpose flour
1¹/2 teaspoons soda
1 teaspoon baking powder
³/4 teaspoon cinnamon
³/4 teaspoon allspice
³/4 teaspoon salt
¹/2 cup butter or margarine,
    softened
3 eggs

1³/4 cups plus 2 tablespoons
    sugar
1¹/2 cups mashed avocados
³/4 cup buttermilk
³/4 cup chopped pecans
¹/2 cup raisins
¹/3 cup sugar
1 teaspoon cinnamon

Preheat oven to 350 degrees. Sift flour, soda, baking powder, ³/4 teaspoon cinnamon, allspice and salt together into bowl. Combine butter, eggs, and 1³/4 cups plus 2 tablespoons sugar in mixer bowl. Beat for 2 minutes. Mix in avocados and buttermilk. Add sifted dry ingredients. Beat for 2 minutes. Stir in pecans and raisins. Pour into 2 greased and floured 5x9-inch loaf pans. Sprinkle with mixture of ¹/3 cup sugar and 1 teaspoon cinnamon. Bake for 1 hour or until loaves test done. Yield: 2 loaves.

Rachel Adams, Ohio

Blueberry Loaf

¹/2 cup melted butter or
    margarine
1 cup sugar
3 eggs
2 teaspoons grated lemon rind
3 cups all-purpose flour

1 teaspoon salt
1 tablespoon baking powder
¹/4 teaspoon soda
1¹/4 cups orange juice
¹/2 cup chopped pecans
1 cup fresh blueberries

Preheat oven to 350 degrees. Combine butter and sugar in bowl. Add eggs and lemon rind; mix well. Combine flour, salt, baking powder and soda. Add to egg mixture alternately with orange juice, mixing well after each addition. Fold in pecans and blueberries. Pour into greased and floured 5x9-inch loaf pan. Bake for 1 hour and 15 minutes or until loaf tests done. Cool in pan for 5 minutes. Remove to wire rack to cool completely. Yield: 1 loaf.

Susanne Motlow, Oklahoma

Brazil Nut Bread

2 cups all-purpose flour
1½ cups sugar
½ teaspoon salt
1 teaspoon baking powder
2 pounds dates, chopped
1 (10-ounce) jar maraschino
    cherries, drained
1 pound Brazil nuts, chopped
8 ounces English walnuts,
    chopped
8 ounces pecans, chopped
½ cup cherry juice
1 teaspoon vanilla extract
4 eggs, beaten
3 tablespoons melted
    shortening

Preheat oven to 300 degrees. Sift flour, sugar, salt and baking powder in bowl. Add dates, cherries, nuts, cherry juice and vanilla; mix well. Stir in eggs and shortening. Spoon into three 5x9-inch loaf pans lined with greased waxed paper. Bake for 1 hour and 30 minutes. Remove to wire rack to cool. Freeze for easier slicing. Yield: 3 loaves.

Connie Maher, Iowa

Bubble Brioche

1 package dry yeast
¼ cup (105 to 115-degree) warm
    water
½ cup butter or margarine,
    softened
⅓ cup sugar
½ teaspoon salt
½ cup milk, scalded, cooled
1 cup all-purpose flour
3 eggs
1 egg yolk
2¼ cups all-purpose flour
1 egg white
1 tablespoon sugar

Dissolve yeast in warm water. Cream butter, ⅓ cup sugar and salt in mixer bowl until light and fluffy. Add milk and 1 cup flour; mix well. Add yeast, eggs and egg yolk; mix well. Add remaining 2¼ cups flour. Beat for 5 to 8 minutes or until very smooth. Let rise, covered, for 2 hours or until doubled in bulk. Stir dough down; beat well. Chill, tightly covered, for 8 hours. Stir dough down. Spoon into greased tube pan in 6 portions. Let rise, covered, for 1 to 2 hours or until doubled in bulk. Preheat oven to 375 degrees. Brush dough with mixture of egg white and 1 tablespoon sugar. Bake for 35 to 45 minutes or until brown. Remove to wire rack to cool. Yield: 12 servings.

Catherine Delaney, Kansas

Candy Cane Coffee Cakes

2 packages dry yeast
1/2 cup warm (105 to 115-
  degree) water
2 cups sour cream
1/4 cup butter or margarine
1/3 cup sugar
2 eggs
2 teaspoons salt
6 cups (about) flour

1 1/2 cups finely chopped dried
  apricots
1 1/2 cups finely chopped
  maraschino cherries
Melted butter or margarine
2 cups confectioners' sugar
2 tablespoons (about) milk
Whole maraschino cherries

Dissolve yeast in 1/2 cup warm water. Heat sour cream in saucepan until lukewarm. Combine sour cream, yeast mixture, 1/4 cup butter, sugar, eggs, salt and 2 cups flour; beat until smooth. Mix in enough remaining flour to make soft dough. Knead on floured surface for 10 minutes. Place in greased bowl, turning to grease surface. Let rise, covered, for 1 hour or until doubled in bulk. Roll into three 6x15-inch rectangles. Place on greased baking sheets. Make 2-inch cuts at 1/2-inch intervals on long sides. Mix apricots and cherries in bowl. Spread mixture down center of each rectangle. Pull up edge strips to cover fruit in crisscross pattern. Stretch dough to 22 inches; shape into candy cane. Let rise until doubled in bulk. Preheat oven to 375 degrees. Bake for 15 to 20 minutes or until golden brown. Brush with melted butter. Blend confectioners' sugar and milk in bowl. Drizzle over coffee cakes. Garnish with whole cherries. Yield: 3 coffee cakes.

Pamela Johnson, Utah

Coconut and Banana Bread

1 1/3 cups flaked coconut
2 3/4 cups all-purpose flour
1 cup sugar
1 tablespoon baking powder

1 tablespoon grated orange rind
1 egg, beaten
1 1/2 cups mashed bananas
1/3 cup milk

Preheat oven to 350 degrees. Sprinkle coconut into shallow baking pan. Bake for 7 to 10 minutes or until lightly toasted, stirring every 2 minutes. Sift flour, sugar and baking powder into bowl. Add coconut and orange rind. Combine egg, bananas and milk in small bowl; mix well. Add to dry ingredients; stir just until moistened. Pour into well-greased and floured 5x9-inch loaf pan. Bake for 1 hour and 10 minutes or until loaf tests done. Cool in pan for 10 minutes. Remove to wire rack to cool completely. Wrap in plastic wrap. Let stand overnight for improved flavor and easier slicing. Slice thinly. Toast if desired. Yield: 1 loaf.

Sarah Thompson, Illinois

Christmas Crown Bread

1 (16-ounce) package country
  white yeast bread mix
2 tablespoons sugar
1/2 cup golden raisins
1/2 cup chopped pecans

1/4 cup chopped dried apricots
1 tablespoon grated lemon rind
1 cup confectioners' sugar
1 to 2 tablespoons water

Preheat oven to 350 degrees. Prepare bread mix according to package directions adding sugar, raisins, pecans, apricots and lemon rind. Knead on lightly floured surface for 5 minutes or until smooth and elastic. Shape into ball. Invert bowl over dough. Let rest for 5 minutes. Reserve 1/3 of the dough. Shape remaining dough into ball; press hole in center and shape as for doughnut. Invert greased 6-ounce custard cup in center of greased baking sheet. Place dough ring over custard cup. Shape reserved dough into two 14-inch ropes; twist ropes together. Place on dough ring and pinch ends together. Let rise, covered with towel, for 50 minutes or until doubled in bulk. Bake for 30 minutes or until golden brown. Cool on wire rack. Loosen custard cup carefully to remove from ring. Drizzle mixture of confectioners' sugar and water over top. Yield: 1 ring.

Frances Ragland, Virginia

Date and Pecan Bread

1 cup chopped dates
1/2 cup Kahlua or orange juice
1/2 cup warm water
1 teaspoon grated orange rind
2/3 cup packed light brown
  sugar

2 tablespoons shortening
1 egg
2 cups sifted all-purpose flour
1 teaspoon soda
1 teaspoon salt
2/3 cup chopped pecans

Preheat oven to 350 degrees. Mix dates, Kahlua, water and orange rind in small bowl. Let stand for 3 minutes. Cream brown sugar, shortening and egg in large bowl until light and fluffy. Sift flour, soda and salt together. Add flour mixture to creamed mixture alternately with date mixture, mixing well after each addition. Stir in chopped pecans. Pour into 3 1/2x10-inch loaf pan. Let stand for 5 minutes. Place on rack just below center of oven. Bake for 60 to 70 minutes or just until loaf tests done in center. Remove to wire rack to cool. Yield: 1 loaf.

Bobbie Wanick, Illinois

Easter Egg Braids

12 eggs	1 cup water
Easter egg dye	1/2 cup sifted all-purpose flour
1 1/2 cups sifted all-purpose flour	Grated rind of 2 lemons
1/2 cup sugar	2 eggs
2 packages dry yeast	2 1/2 cups sifted all-purpose flour
1/2 cup shortening	1 egg, beaten
1/2 cup milk	Candy sprinkles

Tint 12 uncooked eggs with Easter egg dye; set aside. Mix 1 1/2 cups flour, sugar and yeast in mixer bowl. Heat shortening, milk and water to 115 degrees in saucepan. Add to flour mixture. Beat at medium speed for 1 minute. Add 1/2 cup flour, lemon rind and 2 eggs. Beat at high speed for 2 minutes. Stir in enough remaining flour to make medium-stiff dough. Knead on lightly floured surface until smooth and elastic. Place in greased bowl, turning to grease surface. Let rise, covered, in warm place for 1 hour or until doubled in bulk. Punch dough down. Let rise for 30 minutes longer. Shape into four 36-inch ropes. Twist 2 ropes together loosely; shape into ring on greased baking sheet, leaving spaces for 6 tinted eggs. Brush with 1 beaten egg. Insert tinted eggs into spaces. Decorate with sprinkles. Repeat with remaining dough. Preheat oven to 375 degrees. Bake for 20 minutes. Yield: 2 braids.

Donnis Helbourg, Iowa

Ginger Pear Loaves

1 (16-ounce) can Bartlett pears	1 teaspoon ground ginger
1 (18-ounce) package spice cake mix	1/2 cup finely chopped pistachios
4 eggs	1 1/2 cups confectioners' sugar
1/2 cup vegetable oil	2 tablespoons butter or margarine, softened
1 (3 1/2-ounce) package vanilla instant pudding mix	1/8 teaspoon ground ginger

Preheat oven to 350 degrees. Drain pears, reserving liquid. Chop pears. Combine next 6 ingredients and 1/2 cup reserved pear liquid in mixer bowl. Beat at high speed for 2 minutes. Fold in pears. Pour into 5 greased and floured 3x5-inch loaf pans. Bake for 35 minutes or until loaves test done. Cool. Remove from pans. Spread mixture of confectioners' sugar, butter, 1/8 teaspoon ginger and 2 tablespoons reserved pear liquid over tops of loaves. Yield: 5 miniature loaves.

Amanda Traylor, Texas

Eggnog Bread

3/4 cup sugar
2 eggs
1/4 cup melted butter or
    margarine
2 1/4 cups all-purpose flour
2 teaspoons baking powder
1 teaspoon salt

1/8 teaspoon nutmeg
1 cup eggnog
1/2 cup raisins
1/2 cup chopped pecans
1/2 cup chopped candied
    cherries

Preheat oven to 350 degrees. Combine sugar, eggs and butter in mixer bowl. Beat until light. Mix flour, baking powder, salt and nutmeg. Add to sugar mixture alternately with eggnog, mixing well after each addition. Fold in raisins, pecans and cherries. Pour into well-greased and floured 5x9-inch loaf pan. Bake for 1 hour and 10 minutes. Cool in pan for 10 minutes. Remove to wire rack to cool completely. Wrap in plastic wrap. Yield: 1 loaf.

Sonya Isaacs, Louisiana

Holiday Herb Bread

1 cup oats
2 cups boiling water
2 packages dry yeast
1/3 cup warm (105 to 115-
    degree) water
2 1/2 teaspoons salt
1/2 cup molasses

2 tablespoons butter or
    margarine, softened
2 teaspoons sage
1/2 teaspoon caraway seed
1 teaspoon marjoram
6 cups all-purpose flour

Combine oats and boiling water in bowl; mix well. Let stand for 30 minutes. Dissolve yeast in warm water. Add salt, molasses, butter and herbs to oats; mix well. Stir in yeast. Add flour 2 cups at a time, mixing well after each addition. Knead on floured surface for 5 to 10 minutes or until smooth and elastic. Place in greased bowl, turning to grease surface. Let rise, covered, for 2 hours or until doubled in bulk. Punch dough down. Shape into 2 loaves. Place in greased 5x9-inch loaf pans. Let rise, covered, for 1 hour or until doubled in bulk. Preheat oven to 325 degrees. Place loaf pans on rack 4 inches from bottom of oven. Bake for 50 minutes. Remove to wire rack to cool. Yield: 2 loaves.

Bessie Tolliver, Colorado

Nutty Surprise Loaf

2 cups raisins
3 tablespoons orange-flavored
  Brandy
2 cups all-purpose flour
1 package RapidRise yeast
2 tablespoons sugar
1/2 teaspoon salt
1 cup warm (125-degree) water
6 tablespoons butter, softened

1 1/2 to 1 3/4 cups all-purpose
  flour
2 cups finely chopped walnuts
1 1/2 teaspoons cinnamon
1 1/2 teaspoons grated orange
  rind
1 teaspoon grated lemon rind
2 tablespoons melted butter

Preheat oven to 350 degrees. Mix raisins and Brandy in medium bowl. Set aside. Combine 2 cups flour, yeast, sugar and salt in large bowl. Add warm water and 6 tablespoons butter; mix well. Add enough remaining 1 1/2 to 1 3/4 cups flour to make soft dough. Knead dough on lightly floured surface for 8 minutes or until smooth and elastic. Place in greased bowl, turning to grease surface. Let rise, covered, in warm place for 30 minutes or until doubled in bulk. Add walnuts, cinnamon and fruit rinds to raisin mixture; mix well. Divide dough into 3 portions. Roll 1 portion into 12-inch circle on lightly floured surface. Add 1 portion dough to raisin mixture; knead until well mixed. Shape into ball. Place in center of 12-inch circle; bring edge of circle up to enclose ball. Seal edge and smooth surface. Place seam side down in greased 8-inch pie plate. Shape remaining dough into three 10-inch ropes and 6 small balls. Twist each rope into S shape and arrange on top of loaf, crossing in center. Arrange balls on loaf between loops. Pierce loaf through to bottom in many places with ice pick to allow steam to escape. Bake for 1 hour and 15 minutes or until brown. Remove from pie plate to wire rack to cool slightly. Brush with 2 tablespoons melted butter. Cool completely. Yield: 1 loaf.

Wanda Overholzer, Oklahoma

Chocolate Chip Gingerbread

1 (15-ounce) package
  gingerbread mix
1 egg

1 1/4 cups lukewarm water
3/4 cup milk chocolate chips
Vanilla Ice Cream

Preheat oven to 375 degrees. Combine gingerbread mix, egg and water in 8x8-inch cake pan. Mix well with fork. Sprinkle chocolate chips on top. Bake for 30 to 35 minutes. Cool for 15 minutes. Serve warm with vanilla ice cream. Yield: 12 servings.

Jo Ann Jackson, Tennessee

Mincemeat Pecan Loaves

3 cups all-purpose flour
2 cups sugar
2 teaspoons soda
1 teaspoon salt
1 teaspoon baking powder
1 teaspoon cloves
1 teaspoon cinnamon

1 teaspoon nutmeg
2 cups mincemeat
2/3 cups corn oil
1/2 cup apple juice
3 eggs, beaten
2 cups chopped pecans

Preheat oven to 375 degrees. Combine flour, sugar, soda, salt, baking powder and spices in large bowl; mix lightly. Add mincemeat, oil, apple juice, eggs and pecans; stir just until mixed. Pour into 2 greased 5x9-inch loaf pans. Bake for 1 hour or until bread tests done. Cool in pans on wire racks for 10 minutes. Remove to wire racks to cool completely. Wrap loaves individually. Let stand at room temperature for 24 hours or longer before slicing. Yield: 2 loaves.

Barbara Hearn, North Carolina

Orange and Cranberry Bread

1 cup sugar
1/4 cup water
1/2 cup slivered orange rind
1/4 cup butter or margarine
1 cup orange juice
2 eggs, slightly beaten
2 1/2 cups sifted all-purpose
    flour

1 teaspoon baking powder
1/2 teaspoon soda
1 teaspoon salt
1/2 cup wheat germ
1 cup coarsely chopped fresh
    cranberries
1 cup confectioners' sugar
4 1/2 teaspoons milk

Preheat oven to 350 degrees. Line bottoms of 2 greased 5x9-inch loaf pans with greased waxed paper. Combine sugar, water and orange rind in saucepan. Cook over low heat until sugar dissolves, stirring occasionally. Cook for 5 minutes longer, stirring occasionally. Remove from heat. Stir in butter. Cool slightly. Add orange juice and eggs; mix well. Sift flour, baking powder, soda and salt into bowl. Add wheat germ. Add to liquid ingredients, stirring just until moistened. Fold in cranberries. Pour into prepared loaf pans. Let stand for 20 minutes. Bake for 1 hour. Cool in pans for 10 minutes. Remove to wire rack to cool completely. Drizzle with mixture of confectioners' sugar and milk. Yield: 2 loaves.

Connie Bogle, Virginia

Overnight Oatmeal Bread

2 packages dry yeast
1/4 cup sugar
1/2 cup warm (110 to 115-
    degree) water
13/4 cups milk, scalded, cooled
2 tablespoons molasses

3 tablespoons butter or
    margarine, softened
2 teaspoons (or less) salt
5 to 6 cups all-purpose flour
1 cup quick-cooking oats
Vegetable oil

Dissolve yeast and 1 teaspoon sugar in warm water in mixer bowl. Let stand until bubbly. Add remaining sugar, milk, molasses, butter, salt and 2 cups flour. Beat at medium speed until smooth. Add oats and 1 cup flour. Beat until smooth. Mix in enough remaining flour to make soft dough. Knead on floured surface for about 10 minutes or until smooth and elastic. Cover with plastic wrap and towel. Let rest for 10 minutes. Shape into 2 loaves; place in loaf pans. Brush tops with oil; cover with plastic wrap. Chill overnight. Preheat oven to 375 degrees. Let loaves stand at room temperature for 10 minutes. Puncture any large bubbles with toothpick. Bake for 30 to 40 minutes or until brown. Cover with foil to prevent overbrowning if necessary. Yield: 2 loaves.

Margaret Holman, Georgia

Strawberry Bread

3 cups all-purpose flour
1 teaspoon soda
1/2 teaspoon salt
1 teaspoon cinnamon
2 cups sugar
3 eggs, beaten

1 cup oil
3 (10-ounce) packages frozen
    strawberries, thawed
1 cup unsalted butter or
    margarine, softened
1/2 cup confectioners' sugar

Preheat oven to 350 degrees. Combine flour, soda, salt, cinnamon and sugar in bowl. Combine eggs, oil and 2 packages strawberries; mix well. Add to dry ingredients; mix well. Pour into 2 greased and floured 5x9-inch loaf pans. Bake for 1 hour or until loaves test done. Cool in pans for 10 minutes. Remove to wire rack to cool completely. Combine remaining 1 package strawberries, butter and confectioners' sugar in bowl; mix well. Serve with strawberry bread. Yield: 2 loaves.

Gina Marner, Pennsylvania

Miniature Tea Loaves

2 eggs, beaten
2/3 cup milk
2 (7-ounce) packages bran
   muffin mix
1 cup chopped dates

1 cup chopped pecans
8 ounces cream cheese, softened
1/4 cup chopped pecans
1 (8-ounce) can crushed
   pineapple, drained

Preheat oven to 350 degrees. Combine eggs, milk and muffin mix in bowl. Mix just until moistened. Fold in dates and 1 cup pecans. Spoon into 4 greased 2½x4½-inch miniature loaf pans. Bake for 30 minutes or until loaves test done. Cool on wire rack. Combine cream cheese, ¼ cup pecans and pineapple in bowl; mix well. Serve with sliced tea loaves. Yield: 4 miniature loaves.

Jean Bogitch, Oregon

Hot Cross Buns

2 packages dry yeast
1/2 cup warm (105 to 115-
   degree) water
2 cups sour cream
1/4 cup butter or margarine,
   softened
1/3 cup sugar
2 teaspoons salt
2 eggs

2 cups all-purpose flour
1 cup currants
3/4 cup chopped citron
2½ teaspoons cinnamon
1 teaspoon nutmeg
4 cups all-purpose flour
1 egg yolk
Confectioners' sugar frosting

Dissolve yeast in warm water. Heat sour cream to lukewarm over low heat. Combine with yeast, butter, sugar, salt, eggs and 2 cups flour in large bowl. Beat until smooth. Stir in currants, citron and spices. Add remaining 4 cups flour until mixture forms ball, mixing well. Knead on floured surface for 10 minutes or until smooth and elastic. Place in greased bowl, turning to grease surface. Let rise, covered, in warm place for 1 hour or until doubled in bulk. Preheat oven to 375 degrees. Shape dough into 1½-inch balls. Place on greased baking sheet. Brush with egg yolk beaten with a small amount of water. Bake for 20 minutes. Cool. Decorate with frosting cross. Yield: 3 dozen.

Lee McBarron, Indiana

Waldorf Loaf

1 egg, beaten
3/4 cup sugar
1/2 teaspoon vanilla extract
1/2 cup mayonnaise
1 1/2 cups all-purpose flour
1 teaspoon soda
1 teaspoon cinnamon

1/4 teaspoon salt
1/4 cup milk
4 cups chopped unpeeled
   Granny Smith apples
1/2 cup chopped walnuts
1/4 cup finely chopped celery

Preheat oven to 350 degrees. Combine egg, sugar, vanilla and mayonnaise in bowl; mix well. Mix flour, soda, cinnamon and salt. Add to mayonnaise mixture alternately with milk, mixing well after each addition. Fold in apples, walnuts and celery. Pour into well-greased and floured 5x9-inch loaf pan. Bake for 1 hour and 5 minutes or until loaf tests done. Cool in pan for 10 minutes. Remove to wire rack to cool completely. Wrap in plastic wrap. Store in refrigerator. Yield: 1 loaf.

Maxine Flout, West Virginia

English Muffins

1 package dry yeast
2 tablespoons warm (110-
   degree) water
1/2 cup milk, scalded
2 teaspoons sugar

1 cup water
2 cups sifted all-purpose flour
3 tablespoons butter or
   margarine, softened
2 cups sifted all-purpose flour

Dissolve yeast in 2 tablespoons warm water in cup. Let stand for 3 to 5 minutes. Combine milk, sugar and 1 cup water in bowl. Add yeast; mix well. Add 2 cups flour gradually, beating well after each addition. Let rise, covered, in warm place for 1 1/2 hours or until the dough mixture collapses back into bowl. Add 3 tablespoons butter; mix well. Stir and knead in remaining 2 cups flour. Place on surface lightly sprinkled with cornmeal. Let rest for 5 minutes. Pat to 1/2-inch thickness; cut into 3-inch circles. Place on lightly greased baking sheet. Let rise until doubled in bulk. Heat oiled electric skillet to 325 to 350 degrees. Transfer muffins from baking sheet to skillet with pancake turner. Bake for 8 minutes on each side or until light brown. Cool slightly on wire rack.
Yield: 1 1/2 dozen.

Winnette Loomis, Arizona

Pumpkin Muffins

2 cups all-purpose flour
1/2 cup packed dark brown sugar
1 teaspoon soda
1/2 teaspoon cinnamon
1/4 teaspoon ginger
1/8 teaspoon nutmeg

1 cup canned pumpkin
1/2 cup corn oil
2 tablespoons honey
1/2 cup water
1/3 cup coarsely chopped
   walnuts

Preheat oven to 350 degrees. Combine flour, brown sugar, soda and spices in large bowl. Combine pumpkin, oil, honey and water in small bowl; mix well. Add to flour mixture; stir just until moistened. Fold in walnuts. Spoon into greased muffin cups. Bake for 35 minutes or until muffins test done. Remove from pan immediately. Serve warm. Yield: 1 dozen.

Shirley Meyer, Kentucky

Easy One-Rise Caramel Rolls

1 cup packed light brown sugar
1 cup whipping cream
1 package dry yeast
1 cup warm (105 to 115-degree)
   water
1/4 cup sugar
1 3/4 cups bread flour
1 teaspoon salt
1 egg

2 tablespoons melted butter or
   margarine
1 3/4 cups bread flour
1/2 cup sugar
2 teaspoons cinnamon
1 cup chopped walnuts
1/2 cup butter or margarine,
   softened

Mix brown sugar and cream in 10x15-inch baking pan; spread evenly in pan. Dissolve yeast in warm water in cup. Stir in 1/4 cup sugar. Combine with 1 3/4 cups flour, salt, egg, and 2 tablespoons butter in bowl; mix well. Knead in 1 3/4 cups flour until smooth and elastic. Roll into 11x18-inch rectangle on floured surface. Mix 1/2 cup sugar, cinnamon, walnuts and 1/2 cup butter in bowl. Spread over dough. Roll as for jelly roll. Cut into 12 rolls. Arrange in prepared pan. Preheat oven to 200 degrees. Turn off oven. Place pan of hot water on bottom rack of oven. Place rolls on center rack. Let rise until doubled in bulk. Remove pan of water. Set oven temperature at 375 degrees. Bake for 20 minutes. Invert rolls onto serving platter. Yield: 1 dozen.

Gail Cassidy, Florida

Pear Mincemeat Rolls

1 (29-ounce) can Bartlett pears
1 cup prepared mincemeat
4 teaspoons cornstarch
2 teaspoons grated orange rind

2 (8-count) packages
   refrigerator crescent rolls
2 cups confectioners' sugar
4 teaspoons margarine

Preheat oven to 375 degrees. Drain pears, reserving 3 tablespoons liquid. Chop pears finely. Combine chopped pears, mincemeat, cornstarch and orange rind in saucepan. Cook until mixture comes to a boil and thickens, stirring constantly. Cool. Press 1 package roll dough into 13x20-inch rectangle on lightly floured surface, sealing perforations and edges. Spread half the pear mixture on rectangle to within 1/2 inch of edges. Roll as for jelly roll from short end. Cut into 6 slices; arrange cut side down on greased baking sheet. Repeat with remaining roll dough and pear mixture. Bake for 18 to 20 minutes or until golden brown. Combine confectioners' sugar, softened margarine and enough reserved pear liquid to make of glaze consistency in small bowl; mix until smooth. Drizzle over hot rolls. Yield: 1 dozen.

Mary Horn, California

Swirled Chocolate Sweet Rolls

1 package hot roll mix
1 tablespoon sugar
1/4 cup unsweetened baking
   cocoa
1 1/4 cups (120-degree) water
2 tablespoons margarine
1 egg
2 tablespoons margarine

2 tablespoons sugar
1/2 cup miniature chocolate
   chips
Confectioners' sugar
1/4 cup miniature chocolate
   chips
1 teaspoon shortening

Combine yeast and flour from roll mix with 1 tablespoon sugar and cocoa in bowl. Stir in water, 2 tablespoons margarine and egg, mixing until dough pulls from side of bowl. Knead on floured surface until smooth. Cover with large bowl. Let rest for 5 minutes. Roll into 12x15-inch rectangle; spread with 2 tablespoons margarine. Sprinkle with 2 tablespoons sugar and 1/2 cup chocolate chips. Roll up from short end; press edges to seal. Cut into 12 slices. Arrange in greased 9x13-inch baking pan. Let rise, covered, for 30 minutes on wire rack over hot water. Preheat oven to 375 degrees. Bake sweet rolls for 15 to 20 minutes. Sprinkle with confectioners' sugar. Melt 1/4 cup chocolate chips and shortening in saucepan over low heat, stirring to mix well. Drizzle over rolls. Yield: 1 dozen.

Nancy Peek, Mississippi

♥ *Cake Gifts* ♥

Bûche de Noël

4 egg whites
1/4 cup sugar
4 egg yolks
1/2 cup sugar
1/2 cup all-purpose flour
3/4 teaspoon baking powder
1/3 cup unsweetened baking cocoa
1/4 teaspoon salt

1/2 cup confectioners' sugar
1 cup whipping cream
3 tablespoons sugar
1 tablespoon unsweetened baking cocoa
Buttercream Frosting
1/4 cup semisweet chocolate chips
1 teaspoon shortening

Preheat oven to 375 degrees. Line bottom of greased 10x15-inch jelly roll pan with greased waxed paper. Beat egg whites in bowl until soft peaks form. Add 1/4 cup sugar 1 tablespoon at a time, beating until very stiff peaks form. Beat egg yolks and 1/2 cup sugar until very thick. Add flour, baking powder, 1/3 cup cocoa and salt. Beat at low speed until blended. Fold stiffly beaten egg whites gently into batter. Spread batter evenly in prepared pan. Bake for 12 minutes or just until cake springs back when lightly touched. Invert cake onto clean towel sprinkled with confectioners' sugar. Remove waxed paper. Roll cake and towel from narrow end as for jelly roll. Cool on wire rack for 30 minutes. Whip cream with 3 tablespoons sugar and 1 tablespoon cocoa in mixer bowl until stiff. Unroll cake. Spread whipped cream over cake; reroll to enclose filling. Frost with Vanilla Buttercream Frosting. Draw lines and rings with fork to resemble bark. Melt chocolate chips with shortening in double boiler over hot water. Drizzle over cake. Chill until serving time. Yield: 16 servings.

Buttercream Frosting

1 cup butter or margarine, softened
2 cups confectioners' sugar
1 egg yolk

1 tablespoon milk
1 1/2 teaspoons vanilla extract
2 teaspoons unsweetened baking cocoa

Combine all ingredients in mixer bowl. Beat until light and fluffy. Yield: 1 1/2 cups.

Maggie Reynolds, Virginia

Cherry Sweetheart Cake

2½ cups sifted cake flour	2 teaspoons almond extract
1½ cups sugar	1 teaspoon vanilla extract
3½ teaspoons baking powder	4 egg whites
1 teaspoon salt	18 maraschino cherries,
½ cup shortening	chopped
¾ cup milk	½ cup chopped walnuts
⅓ cup maraschino cherry juice	Cherry Sweetheart Frosting

Preheat oven to 375 degrees. Sift flour, sugar, baking powder and salt into mixer bowl. Cut in shortening until crumbly. Mix milk and cherry juice in small bowl. Stir ¾ of the mixture into dry ingredients. Add flavorings. Beat for 2 minutes. Add remaining milk mixture and egg whites. Beat for 2 minutes. Stir in cherries and walnuts. Pour into 2 greased and floured cake pans. Bake for 20 to 25 minutes or until cake tests done. Remove to wire rack to cool. Spread Cherry Sweetheart Frosting between layers and over top and side of cake. Yield: 12 servings.

Cherry Sweetheart Frosting

2 tablespoons shortening	9 tablespoons heavy cream,
2 tablespoons butter	scalded
½ teaspoon almond extract	3½ cups confectioners' sugar
1 teaspoon vanilla extract	Red food coloring
½ teaspoon salt	½ cup finely chopped
½ cup confectioners' sugar	maraschino cherries

Combine shortening, butter, flavorings and salt in mixer bowl; mix well. Beat in ½ cup confectioners' sugar. Add cream alternately with remaining 3½ cups confectioners' sugar, mixing well after each addition. Stir in food coloring and cherries.

Ruth Ann Eccles, Iowa

♥ *For an easy lacy Valentine decoration on an unfrosted cake, place paper doily on top of cake. Sift confectioners' sugar over doily. Remove doily carefully.*

Cherry Chocolate Cake

2 cups all-purpose flour
3/4 cup sugar
1 teaspoon cinnamon
1 teaspoon soda
1 teaspoon salt
3/4 cup vegetable oil
2 eggs

2 teaspoons vanilla extract
1 cup chopped walnuts
1 cup semisweet chocolate chips
1 (22-ounce) can cherry pie
  filling
1 cup confectioners' sugar
2 tablespoons milk

Preheat oven to 350 degrees. Combine flour, sugar, cinnamon, soda and salt in bowl. Add oil, eggs and vanilla; mix well. Stir in walnuts, chocolate chips and pie filling. Pour into greased and floured bundt pan. Bake for 1 hour or until cake tests done. Invert onto cake plate to cool. Blend confectioners' sugar and milk in bowl. Drizzle over cake. Yield: 16 servings.

Kathleen Hamlin, California

Cranberry Tart Cake

2 1/2 cups sifted all-purpose
  flour
1 cup sugar
1 teaspoon soda
1 teaspoon baking powder
1/4 teaspoon salt
Grated rind of 2 oranges
1 cup broken English walnuts

1 cup chopped dates
1 cup chopped cranberries
2 eggs, beaten
1 cup buttermilk
3/4 cup vegetable oil
1 cup orange juice
1 cup sugar

Preheat oven to 350 degrees. Combine flour, 1 cup sugar, soda, baking powder, salt and orange rind in bowl. Mix in walnuts, dates and cranberries. Blend eggs, buttermilk and oil in bowl until smooth. Add to cranberry mixture; stir until well mixed. Spoon into greased and floured tube pan. Bake for 1 hour. Cool in tube pan until lukewarm. Heat orange juice and 1 cup sugar until sugar is dissolved. Remove cake to serving plate. Pour glaze very gradually over cake, allowing cake to absorb mixture. Cool completely. Refrigerate, wrapped in foil, for 24 hours before serving. Yield: 16 servings.

Linda Andrews, Kentucky

Easter Basket Cake

1 (9-inch) sponge cake
Confectioners' sugar icing
3/4 cup sugar
6 tablespoons all-purpose flour
3 eggs
2 1/4 cups milk, scalded
1 teaspoon vanilla extract
1 cup whipping cream, whipped
1/4 cup margarine, softened

1/3 cup sugar
1 egg
1 tablespoon milk
1/2 teaspoon almond extract
1 teaspoon salt
1 1/2 cups all-purpose flour
Large pink, yellow and green
   gumdrops

Preheat oven to 350 degrees. Remove center of cake, leaving 2 inches on bottom and 1 1/2 inches around side. Spread outside and top edge with confectioners' sugar icing. Set aside. Beat 3/4 cup sugar, 6 tablespoons flour and 3 eggs in double boiler until well mixed. Add milk gradually, stirring constantly. Bring to a boil, stirring constantly; remove from heat. Stir in vanilla. Cool, stirring frequently. Fold in whipped cream. Chill, covered, in refrigerator. Cream butter, 1/3 cup sugar and 1 egg in mixer bowl until light. Beat in 1 tablespoon milk, almond extract and salt. Add 1 1/2 cups flour gradually. Shape half the mixture into 18-inch rope. Place on baking sheet in shape of handle for basket cake. Roll remaining dough on floured surface. Cut out bunny or flower shapes. Place on baking sheet. Bake until very light brown. Cool. Fill center of cake with custard. Insert cookie handle into cake. Arrange cookie cutouts on side of cake. Roll gumdrops flat in additional sugar. Cut into flowers and leaves. Arrange on top of cake. Yield: 12 servings.

Linda Austin, Iowa

Apricot Almond Fruitcake Ring

1 cup butter or margarine,
   softened
1 1/4 cups sugar
6 eggs
1 1/4 cups all-purpose flour
1 tablespoon ground cinnamon
1/2 teaspoon ground nutmeg

1/2 teaspoon salt
2 cups golden raisins
1 cup chopped dried apricots
1 cup sliced blanched almonds
8 to 10 dried apricot halves
1/2 cup sliced blanched
   almonds

Preheat oven to 275 degrees. Cream butter and sugar in mixer bowl until light and fluffy. Add eggs 1 at a time, beating well after each addition. Add mixture of flour, spices and salt gradually, mixing well after each addition. Fold in raisins, chopped apricots and 1 cup almonds. Spoon into greased and floured 1-quart ring mold. Bake for 2 hours or until toothpick inserted in center comes out clean. Cool on wire rack for 10 minutes. Loosen edges from side of pan with spatula. Invert onto wire rack to cool completely. Arrange apricot halves and remaining ½ cup almond slices decoratively over top. Store in airtight container. Yield: one 8-inch ring.

Carol Sloan, Kentucky

Candlelight Fruitcake

2½ cups sifted all-purpose flour
1 teaspoon salt
1 teaspoon baking powder
1 teaspoon cinnamon
½ teaspoon nutmeg
½ teaspoon ginger
2 cups chopped pecans
2 cups dark seedless raisins
2 cups golden seedless raisins
1 cup candied cherry halves
2 cups chopped candied pineapple

2 cups chopped mixed candied fruit
1¼ cups shortening
1¼ cups honey
6 eggs
½ cup pecan halves
½ cup whole candied cherries
½ cup mixed dark and golden raisins
½ cup candied pineapple tidbits
½ cup light corn syrup

Preheat oven to 250 degrees. Line bottom of greased 10-inch tube pan with 2 layers of greased waxed paper. Do not use fluted pan. Sift flour, salt, baking powder and spices into bowl. Combine ½ cup sifted mixture with 2 cups pecans and next 5 fruits in bowl; mix well. Cream shortening and honey in mixer bowl until light and fluffy. Add eggs 1 at a time, beating well after each addition. Add remaining sifted mixture; mix well. Fold in floured fruit. Spoon into prepared tube pan. Place shallow pan of hot water on bottom oven rack. Place tube pan on center rack. Bake for 3 hours and 15 minutes. Combine pecan halves, whole cherries, mixed raisins and candied pineapple tidbits in bowl. Bring corn syrup to a boil in saucepan. Cook for 1½ minutes. Add to fruit mixture, toss to coat fruit. Arrange fruit on partially baked fruitcake. Bake for 45 minutes longer or until fruitcake is firm but not dry. Cool completely in pan. Invert onto cake plate; remove waxed paper. Turn cake decorated side up. Store, tightly covered, in refrigerator. Yield: 20 servings.

Lydia Simpson, Texas

♥ *Fruitcakes can be stored indefintely. Wrap them in Brandy or wine-soaked cloths and then in foil. Store in an airtight container in a cool place.*

No Bake Spiced Fruitcake

1/3 cup boiling water
1/2 cup raisins
1/3 cup butter or margarine,
  softened
1/3 cup confectioners' sugar
3 cups graham cracker crumbs
3/4 teaspoon cinnamon
1/4 teaspoon cloves
1/2 teaspoon grated orange rind

1/8 teaspoon salt
1/2 cup honey
11/2 cups chopped dates
11/2 cups chopped red glacéed
  cherries
1 cup chopped walnuts
8 to 10 whole red glacéed
  cherries

Pour boiling water over raisins in bowl. Let stand for 5 minutes; drain well. Set aside. Cream butter and confectioners' sugar in mixer bowl until light and fluffy. Combine graham cracker crumbs, spices, orange rind and salt in bowl; mix well. Add to butter mixture gradually, mixing well after each addition. Add honey; mix well. Add dates, chopped cherries, walnuts and raisins; mix well. Press into greased and foil-lined 4x8-inch loaf cake pan. Chill, wrapped in plastic wrap, for 2 days or longer. Heat unwrapped fruitcake in pan in preheated 500-degree oven for 2 minutes. Loosen edges from pan with spatula; invert onto serving plate. Garnish with whole glacéed cherries. Yield: one 3-pound fruitcake.

Madeline Pickett, Colorado

Italian Cream Cake

1/2 cup butter or margarine,
  softened
1/2 cup shortening
2 cups sugar
5 egg yolks
2 cups all-purpose flour
1 teaspoon soda

1 cup buttermilk
1 teaspoon vanilla extract
1 cup chopped pecans
1 cup flaked coconut
5 egg whites
Cream Cheese Frosting
1 cup flaked coconut

Preheat oven to 350 degrees. Cream butter, shortening and sugar in mixer bowl until light and fluffy. Add egg yolks 1 at a time, beating well after each addition. Add mixture of flour and soda alternately with buttermilk, mixing well after each addition. Blend in vanilla. Fold in pecans and 1 cup coconut. Beat egg whites until stiff peaks form. Fold gently into batter. Pour into 3 greased and floured 8 or 9-inch round cake pans. Bake for 20 to 30 minutes or until layers test done. Cool in pans for 10 minutes. Remove to wire rack to cool completely. Spread Cream Cheese Frosting between layers and over top and side of cake. Sprinkle with 1 remaining cup coconut. Store in refrigerator. Yield: 16 servings.

Cream Cheese Frosting

1/4 cup butter or margarine,
 softened
8 ounces cream cheese, softened
1 egg, beaten

1 1/2 teaspoons vanilla extract
2 (16-ounce) packages
 confectioners' sugar
1 to 2 tablespoons cream

Cream butter, cream cheese, egg and vanilla in mixer bowl until light and fluffy. Add confectioners' sugar gradually, beating well after each addition. Add enough cream to make of desired spreading consistency.

Velma Sikes, Tennessee

Old-Fashioned Jam Cake

2 cups sugar
4 eggs
1 teaspoon allspice
1 teaspoon cinnamon
1 teaspoon nutmeg
1 cup peach preserves
1 cup strawberry preserves
1 cup pear preserves

1 cup blackberry jam
1 cup seedless raisins
1 cup chopped nuts
1 1/2 cups sour cream
1 tablespoon soda
4 cups all-purpose flour
1 cup buttermilk
Creamy Caramel Icing

Preheat oven to 325 degrees. Line 5 waxed 8-inch round cake pans with greased waxed paper. Combine sugar, eggs and spices in mixer bowl. Beat until light and fluffy. Add preserves, jam, raisins and nuts; mix well. Combine sour cream and soda. Add to jam mixture alternately with flour and buttermilk, mixing well after each addition. Pour into prepared cake pans. Bake for 35 to 45 minutes or until layers test done. Cool in pans for 10 minutes. Invert onto wire rack to cool completely. Frost with Creamy Caramel Icing. Yield: 16 servings.

Creamy Caramel Icing

2 cups butter or margarine
4 cups packed light brown sugar
1 cup milk

8 cups (about) sifted
 confectioners' sugar

Melt butter in saucepan. Stir in brown sugar. Bring to a boil. Cook over low heat for 2 minutes, stirring constantly. Stir in milk. Bring to a boil, stirring constantly. Cool to lukewarm. Add confectioners' sugar. Beat until of spreading consistency.

Gail O'Malley, Kansas

Mocha Cake

2 cups sugar
1/2 cup shortening
1/2 cup unsweetened baking
   cocoa
1 teaspoon vanilla extract
1 cup boiling water
1/2 cup buttermilk

2 eggs
2 cups sifted all-purpose flour
1/4 teaspoon salt
1 1/4 teaspoons soda
Mocha Frosting
Chocolate Leaves

Preheat oven to 350 degrees. Cream sugar, shortening, cocoa and vanilla in mixer bowl until light and fluffy. Add water gradually, mixing well after each addition. Stir in buttermilk and eggs. Sift remaining ingredients together. Add to batter gradually, mixing well after each addition. Pour into 2 greased and floured 8-inch round cake pans. Bake for 30 minutes or until cake tests done. Cool in pan for 10 minutes. Remove to wire rack to cool completely. Spread Mocha Frosting between layers and over top and side of cake. Decorate top of cake with Chocolate Leaves. Yield: 12 servings.

Mocha Frosting

1/3 cup semisweet chocolate
   chips
1 cup butter or margarine,
   softened

3 egg yolks
1/4 cup strong black coffee
6 cups sifted confectioners'
   sugar

Melt chocolate chips in double boiler over hot water. Cream butter in mixer bowl until light. Add egg yolks and coffee. Beat until blended. Add confectioners' sugar gradually, beating well after each addition. Add chocolate; mix well. Yield: 3 cups.

Chocolate Leaves

1 cup semisweet chocolate chips   1 cup rose leaves

Melt chocolate chips in double boiler over hot water. Wash rose leaves; pat dry. Brush chocolate over back of each leaf. Place on waxed-paper lined tray. Chill until firm. Peel off leaves carefully. Store in refrigerator.

Evelyn Braden, Nebraska

Orange Crown Cake

8 egg whites, at room
  temperature
1/4 teaspoon salt
1/2 cup sugar
1 cup butter or margarine,
  softened
11/2 cups sugar
1 teaspoon vanilla extract
3 cups all-purpose flour

1 tablespoon baking powder
1 cup orange juice
1 teaspoon grated orange rind
Orange Frosting
20 pecan halves
15 candied cherry halves
Sections of 2 fresh oranges
1/4 cup coconut

Preheat oven to 350 degrees. Beat egg whites with salt in mixer bowl until soft peaks form. Add 1/2 cup sugar gradually, beating until stiff and glossy. Set aside. Cream butter, 11/2 cups sugar and vanilla in mixer bowl until light and fluffy. Mix flour and baking powder in bowl. Add flour mixture to creamed mixture alternately with orange juice, mixing well after each addition. Stir in orange rind. Fold in egg whites gently. Spoon into 3 greased and floured 9-inch cake pans. Bake for 20 to 25 minutes, or until golden brown. Cool in pans for 5 minutes. Remove to wire rack to cool completely. Spread Orange Frosting with fruit and nuts between layers and on side of cake. Spread reserved smooth Orange Frosting on top of cake. Garnish top of cake with pecan halves, cherry halves, orange sections and coconut. Store, covered, in refrigerator.
Yield: 12 to 16 servings.

Orange Frosting

8 egg yolks, beaten
11/4 cups sugar
1/2 cup butter or margarine
2 teaspoons grated orange rind
3/4 cup chopped pecans

3/4 cup shredded coconut
3/4 cup chopped candied
  cherries
Sections of 2 fresh oranges,
  chopped

Combine egg yolks, sugar, butter and orange rind in double boiler. Cook over simmering water for 10 minutes or until mixture is almost translucent and mounds when dropped from spoon, stirring constantly. Remove from heat. Cool to room temperature. Reserve 1/4 of the mixture in small bowl. Combine remaining mixture with pecans, coconut, cherries and oranges in bowl; mix gently. Chill both mixtures, covered, for several hours or until of spreading consistency.

Frances Palmer, Indiana

Fuzzy Navel Cake

1 (18-ounce) package white
   cake mix
1 (8-ounce) container orange
   yogurt
1 (8-ounce) container peach
   yogurt
1/3 cup vegetable oil
3/4 cup peach schnapps or
   peach nectar

2 eggs
1 (8-ounce) jar orange
   marmalade
1/2 cup peach schnapps or
   peach nectar
2 tablespoons sugar
1 (8-ounce) container whipped
   topping
4 ounces cream cheese, softened

Preheat oven to 350 degrees. Combine cake mix, yogurts, oil, 3/4 cup
schnapps and eggs in large mixer bowl. Beat at high speed for 3 minutes.
Pour into 2 greased and floured 9-inch cake pans. Bake for 35 minutes or
until cake tests done. Remove to wire rack to cool. Heat marmalade, 1/2
cup schnapps and 2 tablespoons sugar in saucepan until bubbly. Cool
completely. Spread between cake layers. Beat whipped topping and
cream cheese in mixer bowl at high speed for 3 minutes. Spread over top
and side of cake. Yield: 12 servings.

Polly Nelson, West Virginia

Chocolate and Apricot Torte

3 tablespoons toasted bread
   crumbs
1/3 cup orange juice
11/4 cups dried apricots
3/4 cup unsweetened butter,
   softened
1 cup sugar
5 eggs
1 cup semisweet chocolate
   chips, melted
11/2 teaspoons vanilla extract

2/3 cup toasted fine bread
   crumbs
1 tablespoon all-purpose flour
11/2 cups chopped pecans
1/4 cup unsweetened baking
   cocoa
1/4 cup sugar
1/4 cup heavy cream
2 tablespoons butter or
   margarine
15 pecan halves

Preheat oven to 375 degrees. Sprinkle 3 tablespoons bread crumbs into
buttered 9-inch springform pan. Heat orange juice just to the simmering
point in saucepan over medium heat. Remove from heat. Stir in apricots.
Let stand for 15 minutes. Cream 3/4 cup butter and 1 cup sugar in mixer
bowl until light. Blend in eggs 1 at a time. Add melted chocolate chips,
vanilla and 2/3 cup bread crumbs; mix well. Stir in flour and chopped
pecans. Drain apricots. Fold into batter. Spoon into prepared pan. Bake
for 50 to 60 minutes or until toothpick inserted in center comes out clean.
Cool in pan on wire rack. Combine cocoa, 1/4 cup sugar, cream and 2

tablespoons butter in small saucepan. Heat over low heat until smooth, stirring constantly. Place torte on serving plate; remove side of pan. Spoon glaze over torte, smoothing with spatula. Arrange pecan halves on top. Chill, wrapped, for several hours to several days. Let stand at room temperature for 20 minutes before serving. Yield: 16 servings.

Natalie Northcutt, Minnesota

Christmas Torte

4 egg yolks
1/3 cup sugar
1/4 cup water
1 teaspoon vanilla extract
1/2 cup all-purpose flour
1/3 cup unsweetened baking
    cocoa
1/4 teaspoon soda

1/2 teaspoon baking powder
1/8 teaspoon salt
4 egg whites
1/2 cup sugar
Creamy Ricotta Filling
Chocolate Glaze
1/4 cup sliced almonds
1/2 cup candied red cherries

Preheat oven to 350 degrees. Line 10x15-inch baking pan with greased foil. Combine egg yolks, 1/3 cup sugar, water and vanilla in mixer bowl. Beat at high speed for 5 minutes or until thick and lemon-colored. Mix flour, cocoa, soda, baking powder and salt in small bowl. Add to egg yolk mixture, beating at low speed just until blended. Beat egg whites in large mixer bowl until foamy. Add 1/2 cup sugar gradually, beating until stiff peaks form. Fold in chocolate mixture gently. Spoon evenly into prepared pan. Bake for 12 to 15 minutes or until top springs back when lightly touched. Invert onto wire rack. Remove foil carefully. Cool completely. Cut crosswise into four 3³/₄x10-inch strips. Spread Creamy Ricotta Filling between layers. Spoon Chocolate Glaze (page 32) over top of cake. Garnish with sliced almonds and candied cherries. Chill for several hours. Yield: 10 servings.

Creamy Ricotta Filling

1/2 cup whipping cream
1 cup ricotta cheese
1/3 cup confectioners' sugar
1/3 cup chopped candied
    cherries

1/4 cup miniature semisweet
    chocolate chips
1/2 teaspoon vanilla extract
1/4 teaspoon almond extract

Whip cream in mixer bowl until soft peaks form. Beat ricotta cheese and confectioners' sugar in mixer bowl at high speed until smooth. Fold in whipped cream, cherries, chocolate chips and extracts.

Helen Eagleton, Oklahoma

Chocolate Glaze

2 tablespoons butter or
  margarine
2 tablespoons unsweetened
  baking cocoa

2 tablespoons water
1 cup confectioners' sugar
1/2 teaspoon vanilla extract

Melt butter in small saucepan over low heat. Add cocoa and water. Cook over low heat until mixture thickens, stirring constantly; do not boil. Cool slightly. Add confectioners' sugar and vanilla; mix well.

Helen Eagleton, Oklahoma

Strawberry and Sour Cream Cake

2 cups all-purpose flour
1 teaspoon soda
1/3 teaspoon salt
1 1/4 cups sugar
1/2 cup shortening
3 eggs
1/2 cup sour cream

1 teaspoon vanilla extract
1 (16-ounce) package frozen
  strawberries, thawed, drained
Creamy Frosting
Mint leaves
Fresh strawberries

Preheat oven to 350 degrees. Sift flour, soda, salt and sugar into mixer bowl. Add shortening, eggs, sour cream and vanilla. Beat at low speed for 3 minutes. Beat at high speed for 3 minutes. Fold in strawberries. Spoon into 2 greased and floured 8-inch cake pans. Bake for 30 to 40 minutes. Cool in pans for 10 minutes. Remove to wire rack to cool completely. Spread Creamy Frosting between layers and over top and side of cake. Garnish with mint leaves and fresh strawberries. Yield: 12 servings.

Creamy Frosting

1/2 cup shortening
1/2 cup butter or margarine,
  softened
3 tablespoons all-purpose flour

1 teaspoon vanilla extract
2 tablespoons strawberry juice
2 cups confectioners' sugar

Cream shortening and butter in mixer bowl until light and fluffy. Add flour, vanilla, strawberry juice and confectioners' sugar. Beat for 7 minutes or until of spreading consistency.

Peggy Garrett, Florida

Treasure Toffee Cake

1/4 cup sugar
1 teaspoon cinnamon
2 cups all-purpose flour
1 cup sugar
1 cup sour cream
2 eggs
1/2 cup butter or margarine,
  softened

1 1/2 teaspoons soda
1/4 teaspoon salt
1 teaspoon vanilla extract
1/4 cup chopped pecans
3 (1 1/8-ounce) chocolate toffee
  candy bars, crushed
1/4 cup melted butter
Confectioners' sugar

Preheat oven to 325 degrees. Mix 1/4 cup sugar and cinnamon in cup. Set aside. Combine flour, 1 cup sugar, sour cream, eggs, 1/2 cup butter, soda, salt and vanilla in mixer bowl. Beat at low speed until moistened. Beat at medium speed for 3 minutes. Layer batter and cinnamon-sugar 1/2 at a time in greased and floured tube pan. Sprinkle with pecans and candy. Pour melted butter over top. Bake for 45 minutes. Cool in pan for 15 minutes. Remove to wire to rack to cool completely. Dust with confectioners' sugar. Yield: 16 servings.

Patricia Boord, Missouri

Irish Cream Cheesecake

1 1/2 cups graham cracker
  crumbs
1/2 cup sugar
6 tablespoons melted butter or
  margarine
1 small package French vanilla
  pudding and pie filling mix
1/3 cup sugar
1 cup Irish cream liqueur

1/2 cup milk
24 ounces cream cheese,
  softened
3 eggs
1 tablespoons Irish cream
  liqueur
1 cup sour cream
3/4 cup confectioners' sugar

Preheat oven to 375 degrees. Mix graham cracker crumbs, 1/2 cup sugar and butter in bowl. Press into bottom and 2 1/2 inches up side of greased springform pan. Blend pudding, 1/3 cup sugar, 1 cup liqueur and milk in saucepan. Cook until thickened and bubbly. Spoon into bowl to cool. Beat cream cheese in mixer bowl until fluffy. Beat in eggs. Beat in pudding mixture. Pour into crust. Bake for 50 minutes. Blend 1 tablespoon liqueur, sour cream and confectioners' sugar in bowl. Spread over top. Bake for 2 minutes longer. Yield: 12 servings.

Barbara Bernhard, Nevada

Christmas Cheesecake

1 cup sifted all-purpose flour
1 teaspoon grated lemon rind
1/4 cup sugar
3/4 teaspoon vanilla extract
1 egg yolk
1/4 cup butter or margarine, softened
1 3/4 cups sugar
40 ounces cream cheese, softened
1 1/2 teaspoons grated lemon rind
1 1/2 teaspoons grated orange rind
3 tablespoons all-purpose flour
1/4 teaspoon vanilla extract
5 eggs
2 egg yolks
1/4 cup whipping cream
1 cup sugar
1 tablespoon cornstarch
1/2 cup water
1 1/2 cups cranberries

Combine 1 cup flour, 1 teaspoon lemon rind and 1/4 cup sugar in bowl. Add 3/4 teaspoon vanilla, 1 egg yolk and butter; mix well. Shape into ball; wrap in plastic wrap. Chill for 1 hour. Preheat oven to 400 degrees. Press 1/3 of the chilled dough over bottom of 10-inch springform pan. Remove side of pan. Bake for 8 minutes. Cool. Replace side of pan. Press remaining dough over side of pan to within 1 inch of top. Chill in refrigerator. Increase oven temperature to 500 degrees. Cream 1 3/4 cups sugar and cream cheese in mixer bowl until light and fluffy. Add grated rinds, 3 tablespoons flour and 1/4 teaspoon vanilla; mix well. Add eggs and 2 egg yolks 1 at a time, beating well after each addition. Add cream; mix well. Pour into prepared pan. Bake for 10 minutes. Reduce oven temperature to 250 degrees. Bake for 1 hour longer. Cool in pan on wire rack. Combine 1 cup sugar, cornstarch and water in saucepan. Add cranberries. Cook over low heat until thickened, stirring constantly. Simmer for 2 minutes. Cool. Spread over cheesecake. Chill, covered, for 3 hours or longer. Place on serving plate; remove side of pan.
Yield: 16 servings.

Sonya Holdman, Illinois

Sweetheart Chocolate Cheesecake

1 1/2 cups miniature semisweet chocolate chips
11 ounces cream cheese, softened
1/3 cup sugar
1/4 cup butter or margarine, softened
1 1/2 teaspoons vanilla extract
3/4 cup chopped pecans
1 cup whipping cream
1 4-ounce milk chocolate bar
2 tablespoons water
1/2 cup whipping cream
2 tablespoons confectioners' sugar
1/2 teaspoon vanilla extract
Semisweet chocolate curls

Melt chocolate chips in double boiler. Combine cream cheese, sugar and butter in large mixer bowl; beat until smooth. Add 1½ teaspoons vanilla. Beat in melted chocolate and pecans. Whip 1 cup heavy cream in bowl until stiff peaks form. Fold into chocolate mixture. Spoon into foil-lined 5-cup heart-shaped mold. Chill until firm. Unmold onto serving tray; peel off foil. Chill in refrigerator. Melt milk chocolate bar in water in double boiler, stirring occasionally. Cool slightly. Spread over mold. Combine ½ cup cream, confectioners' sugar and ½ teaspoon vanilla in small mixer bowl. Beat until stiff peaks form. Frost side of mold. Chill until serving time. Decorate top with chocolate curls. Yield: 12 servings.

Melanie Sturges, Pennsylvania

Pumpkin Cheesecake

2½ cups graham cracker
  crumbs
½ cup melted butter or
  margarine
2 tablespoons sugar
½ teaspoon cinnamon
1 envelope unflavored gelatin
¾ cup pineapple juice
1 (16-ounce) can pumpkin
1 cup packed light brown sugar
3 eggs, beaten

1 teaspoon cinnamon
½ teaspoon ginger
16 ounces cream cheese,
  softened
1 tablespoon vanilla extract
1 cup whipping cream
1 (20-ounce) can crushed
  pineapple, drained
½ cup miniature
  marshmallows

Preheat oven to 350 degrees. Combine graham cracker crumbs, butter, sugar and ½ teaspoon cinnamon in bowl; mix well. Press mixture over bottom and 1½ inches up side of springform pan. Bake for 10 minutes. Cool on wire rack. Soften gelatin in pineapple juice in saucepan. Add pumpkin, brown sugar, eggs, cinnamon and ginger; mix well. Simmer, covered, for 30 minutes, stirring occasionally. Beat cream cheese with vanilla in mixer bowl until fluffy. Add to warm pumpkin mixture, stirring just until blended. Pour into prepared springform pan. Chill, covered, for 8 hours. Whip cream in mixer bowl until stiff. Fold in pineapple and marshmallows gently. Spoon over cheesecake. Chill until serving time. Remove side of pan. Yield: 16 servings.

Lucille Moran, Alabama

Cherry Valentine Cheesecake

2 cups graham cracker crumbs
3 tablespoons sugar
6 tablespoons butter or
 margarine, softened
4 eggs
1 cup sugar
24 ounces cream cheese,
 softened

1 teaspoon vanilla extract
2 teaspoons lemon juice
1 cup sour cream
2 tablespoons sugar
1/2 teaspoon vanilla extract
1 (22-ounce) can cherry pie
 filling

Preheat oven to 375 degrees. Mix cracker crumbs, 3 tablespoons sugar and butter in bowl. Press over bottom and up side to within 1 inch of top of springform pan. Beat eggs in mixer bowl until fluffy. Beat in 1 cup sugar gradually. Add cream cheese, 1 teaspoon vanilla, and lemon juice; beat until smooth. Pour into prepared pan. Bake for 30 to 35 minutes. Cool for 1 hour. Increase oven temperature to 400 degrees. Combine sour cream, 2 tablespoons sugar and 1/2 teaspoon vanilla in bowl. Spread over cheesecake. Bake for 15 minutes; cool. Chill in refrigerator. Top with pie filling. Place on serving plate; remove side of pan. Yield: 12 servings.

Deb Tornholm, Iowa

White Christmas Cheesecake

1½ cups graham cracker
 crumbs
5 tablespoons melted butter or
 margarine
1 tablespoon sugar
32 ounces cream cheese,
 softened
1/2 cup butter or margarine,
 softened

4 eggs
10 ounces white chocolate,
 melted
4½ teaspoons vanilla extract
1 cup sugar
1 cup sour cream
1/4 cup sugar
1 teaspoon vanilla extract
Fresh strawberries

Mix cracker crumbs, melted butter and 1 tablespoon sugar in bowl. Press into 9-inch springform pan. Chill for several hours. Preheat oven to 350 degrees. Combine cream cheese and 1/2 cup butter in mixer bowl; beat until smooth. Blend in eggs 1 at a time, mixing well after each addition. Add chocolate, 4½ teaspoons vanilla and 1 cup sugar; beat for 2 minutes. Pour into prepared pan. Bake for 1 hour. Mix sour cream, 1/4 cup sugar and 1 teaspoon vanilla in bowl. Spread over baked layer. Bake for 10 to 15 minutes or until topping is set. Turn off oven. Let cheesecake stand in closed oven for 2 hours. Chill overnight. Place on serving plate. Remove side of pan. Garnish with strawberries. Yield: 12 servings.

Diana Golf, Mississippi

Tutti-Frutti Chocolate Delight

3/4 cup superfine sugar
1 1/4 cups sifted cake flour
1 cup egg whites, at room
  temperature
1/4 teaspoon salt
1 teaspoon cream of tartar
3/4 cup superfine sugar

1/2 teaspoon almond extract
Apricot Filling
2 (3-ounce) bars Swiss dark
  chocolate
1/2 cup sour cream
2 1/2 cups confectioners' sugar

Preheat oven to 325 degrees. Sift 3/4 cup superfine sugar and cake flour together 4 times; set aside. Beat egg whites and salt at medium speed in mixer bowl for 2 minutes. Add cream of tartar. Beat at high speed until soft peaks form. Add remaining 3/4 cup superfine sugar 1/4 cup at a time, beating at high speed until very stiff peaks form. Fold in almond flavoring. Fold in flour mixture gently 1/4 cup at a time. Spoon into floured 10-inch tube pan; do not grease pan. Cut through with knife. Bake for 50 minutes or until brown and dry. Turn off oven. Let cake stand in closed oven for 10 minutes. Invert tube pan on funnel to cool. Remove cake from pan; split into 2 layers. Spread Apricot Filling between layers. Melt dark chocolate in double boiler over hot water. Stir in 1/2 cup sour cream and confectioners' sugar gradually. Add enough hot water 1 tablespoon at a time to make of desired consistency. Drizzle over outer edge and side of cake. Let stand for 15 minutes. May be baked in 10-inch springform pan with removable center if cake with straight sides is preferred. Yield: 12 servings.

Apricot Filling

1 (3 1/2-ounce) bar Swiss milk
  chocolate with apricot filling,
  chopped
1/2 cup sour cream

1 cup dried apricots, finely
  chopped
1 cup whipping cream, whipped

Combine milk chocolate bar, 1/2 cup sour cream and apricots in bowl; mix well. Fold in whipped cream gently. Yield: 2 cups.

Lannie Seals, Tennessee

Shamrock Cake

1 (2-layer) package white
     cake mix
1/4 cup green Crème de Menthe
1 (16-ounce) jar fudge ice
     cream topping

3 tablespoons green Crème
     de Menthe
1 tablespoon white Crème
     de Cacao
12 ounces whipped topping

Prepare and bake cake mix using package directions for 9x13-inch cake pan, adding 1/4 cup Crème de Menthe. Spread fudge topping over warm cake. Cool. Blend 3 tablespoons Crème de Menthe and Crème de Cacao into whipped topping. Spread over cake. Yield: 15 servings.

Myrt Combs, Idaho

Filled Chocolate Valentine Cake

1 1/2 cups sour cream
1 3/4 cups all-purpose flour
1 3/4 cups sugar
3/4 cup unsweetened baking
     cocoa
1 1/2 teaspoons soda
1 teaspoon salt
2/3 cup butter, softened
2 eggs
1 teaspoon vanilla extract

1/4 cup all-purpose flour
1/2 cup milk
1/4 cup butter, softened
1/4 cup shortening
2 teaspoons vanilla extract
1/4 teaspoon salt
4 cups confectioners' sugar
Chocolate Glaze
1 can chocolate decorator's
     frosting

Heat sour cream in saucepan to lukewarm. Combine next 5 dry ingredients in mixer bowl. Blend in sour cream, 2/3 cup butter, eggs and 1 teaspoon vanilla at low speed. Beat at medium speed for 3 minutes. Pour into 2 greased and floured heart-shaped layer cake pans. Bake at 350 degrees for 30 minutes or until cake tests done. Cool in pan for 10 minutes. Invert onto wire racks to cool completely. Combine remaining 1/4 cup flour and milk in saucepan. Cook until thickened, stirring constantly with wire whisk. Cool. Cream remaining 1/4 cup butter and shortening in mixer bowl until light and fluffy. Add cooked mixture, remaining 2 teaspoons vanilla, salt and confectioners' sugar; mix well. Split cake layers. Place 1 layer cut side down on cake plate. Spread with 1/3 of the filling. Repeat with remaining layers and filling, ending with cake. Pour Chocolate Glaze (page 32) over top. Garnish with chocolate decorator's frosting and almonds if desired. Yield: 8 to 10 servings.

Photograph for this recipe is on the cover.

♥ *Candy Gifts* ♥

Forever Ambers

1 (16-ounce) package orange
  slice candy, chopped
1 (14-ounce) can sweetened
  condensed milk

1 cup chopped pecans
1 (4-ounce) can flaked coconut
1 teaspoon orange extract
2 cups confectioners' sugar

Preheat oven to 300 degrees. Combine orange candy, condensed milk, pecans, coconut and orange extract in bowl; mix well. Spoon into baking dish. Bake for 20 minutes or until mixture bubbles. Stir in confectioners' sugar until smooth. Drop by teaspoonfuls onto waxed paper-lined surface. Let stand until firm. Yield: 2 dozen.

Wanda Stetson, Texas

Aunt Bill's Brown Candy

6 cups sugar
2 cups evaporated milk
1/2 teaspoon soda

1/2 cup butter or margarine
1 teaspoon vanilla extract
2 pounds pecans

Cook 2 cups sugar in heavy skillet over low heat for 30 minutes or until caramelized, stirring constantly with wooden spoon. Combine 4 cups sugar and evaporated milk in saucepan. Bring to a boil. Add caramelized sugar gradually, stirring constantly. Cook to 250 degrees on candy thermometer, hard-ball stage. Remove from heat. Stir in soda vigorously. Add butter. Let stand for 20 minutes. Add vanilla. Beat until mixture loses its luster. Stir in pecans. Pour onto buttered baking sheet. Cool slightly. Cut into squares. Yield: 6 pounds.

Willie Cook, Kansas

♥ *Make easy Christmas candies by melting 1 cup chocolate chips and 1/2 cup butterscotch chips together. Stir in 3 ounces chow mein noodles and drop onto waxed paper. Shape into 2-inch V-shaped "Rudolph's Antlers" candies. Place 1/2 maraschino cherry in center of each and chill until set.*

Chocolate Brittle

1 cup sugar	1 teaspoon vanilla extract
1/2 cup light corn syrup	1/2 teaspoon soda
1/2 cup whole pecans	1/2 cup chocolate chips
2 tablespoons margarine	1/2 cup coarsely chopped pecans

Combine sugar and corn syrup in 2-quart glass bowl. Microwave on High in 700-watt microwave oven for 6 minutes, stirring once. Add whole pecans, margarine and vanilla; mix well. Microwave for 1 minute longer. Stir in soda. Spread on foil-lined surface. Sprinkle chocolate chips over hot candy. Let stand for 1 1/2 minutes. Spread chocolate over top. Sprinkle with chopped pecans. Chill until firm. Break into pieces. Yield: 1 pound.

Flossie Bentson, North Dakota

Microwave Peanut Brittle

1 cup raw peanuts	1 tablespoon butter or
1 cup sugar	margarine
1/8 teaspoon salt	1 teaspoon vanilla extract
1/2 cup light corn syrup	1 teaspoon soda

Combine first 4 ingredients in glass bowl. Microwave on High for 2 to 8 minutes, stirring once. Add butter and vanilla. Microwave for 1 to 2 minutes longer or until peanuts are brown. Stir in soda. Pour onto buttered baking sheet. Cool for 30 minutes. Break into pieces. Yield: 1 pound.

Sandra Crosby, Michigan

Peanut Brittle

1 cup raw peanuts	2 tablespoons water
1 cup sugar	1 tablespoon light corn syrup
1/2 cup melted margarine	1/8 teaspoon vanilla extract

Preheat oven to 300 degrees. Spread peanuts on baking sheet. Place in oven to warm. Combine sugar, margarine, water and corn syrup in 2-quart saucepan. Cook to 275 degrees on candy thermometer, soft-crack stage; do not stir. Add warm peanuts and vanilla. Pour onto foil-lined tray. Let stand until cool. Break into pieces. Yield: 1 pound.

Cindy Lewis, Arkansas

Caramel Butterflies

1 pound caramels
3 tablespoons whipping cream
1 tablespoon butter or
  margarine

3 cups Jordan almonds
12 ounces semisweet chocolate
2 tablespoons shortening
Candy sprinkles

Combine caramels, cream and butter in double boiler. Cook over hot water until caramels melt and are smooth and creamy, stirring constantly. Shape 1 teaspoon mixture into ball. Insert 4 almonds into caramel ball to resemble butterfly wings. Flatten slightly on foil-covered surface. Repeat until all caramel is used. Cool. Melt chocolate with shortening in double boiler over hot water, stirring constantly. Cool slightly. Spread chocolate over caramel, leaving almond wings uncovered. Decorate with sprinkles. Cool. Store in airtight container. Yield: 4 dozen.

Lucy McIntosh, Iowa

Cherry Candy Apples

2 cups sugar
2/3 cup red maraschino cherry
  syrup
3/4 cup hot water

3/4 teaspoon red food coloring
8 medium red apples on
  wooden skewers

Dissolve sugar in syrup and 3/4 cup water. Add food coloring. Cook over medium heat to 300 degrees on candy thermometer. Remove from heat. Twirl apples in hot syrup until completely covered; drain over saucepan. Place on foil-lined tray. Let stand until cool. Yield: 8 servings.

Lisa Addison, Indiana

Chocolate-Covered Cherries

1 pound bitter chocolate
1/2 ounce paraffin
1 (16-ounce) package
  confectioners' sugar

3 tablespoons evaporated milk
1 teaspoon vanilla extract
1 large jar maraschino cherries
  with stems, drained

Melt chocolate and paraffin in double boiler; cool slightly. Mix confectioners' sugar, evaporated milk and vanilla in bowl. Shape into half-dollar sized circles. Wrap around cherry. Dip by stem into chocolate to coat. Cool on waxed paper for 2 hours. Yield: 5 dozen.

Marian Hart, West Virginia

Cherry Mash Balls

1 (16-ounce) package
  confectioners' sugar
1/4 cup melted butter or
  margarine
1 (11-ounce) package cherry
  frosting mix
1/3 (14-ounce) can sweetened
  condensed milk

2 teaspoons vanilla extract
1 (4-ounce) jar maraschino
  cherries, drained, chopped
1 (12-ounce) package milk
  chocolate chips
1 ounce paraffin, chopped
8 ounces peanuts, ground

Combine confectioners' sugar, butter, frosting mix, condensed milk and vanilla in bowl; mix until smooth and creamy. Add chopped cherries to frosting mixture; mix well. Chill until firm enough to handle. Shape into small balls. Place in single layer on foil-covered tray. Freeze until firm. Combine chocolate chips and paraffin in double boiler. Heat over hot water until melted, stirring constantly. Stir in peanuts. Dip candy balls into chocolate mixture to coat; place on foil-lined tray. Let stand until cool. Store in covered container in refrigerator. Yield: 3 pounds.

Donna Wilborne, Arizona

Divinity Kisses

2 1/3 cups sugar
1/2 cup light corn syrup
1/4 teaspoon salt
1/2 cup water

2 egg whites
1 teaspoon vanilla extract
1/2 cup chopped pecans
30 milk chocolate kisses

Combine sugar, corn syrup, salt and water in heavy 2-quart saucepan. Bring to a boil over medium heat, stirring until sugar dissolves. Cook, covered, over high heat for 2 to 3 minutes or until steam washes sugar crystals from side of pan. Cook, uncovered, to 260 degrees on candy thermometer, hard-ball stage; do not stir. Beat egg whites in mixer bowl until stiff peaks form. Add hot syrup to egg whites, beating constantly until stiff. Beat in vanilla. Mix in pecans. Drop by teaspoonfuls onto waxed paper. Press chocolate kiss into center of each. Let stand until cool. Store in airtight container. Yield 2 1/2 dozen.

Delores Whisenant, California

Chocolate-Dipped Dried Fruits

12 ounces semisweet chocolate,
  milk chocolate or white
  chocolate
2 tablespoons shortening

12 ounces dried fruits such as
  apricots, pears, peaches or
  pineapple

Melt chocolate and shortening in double boiler over hot water, stirring to mix well. Dip 1 piece of fruit at a time into chocolate, coating halfway; allow excess chocolate to drip into double boiler. Place on waxed paper; let stand until firm. Place in bonbon cups. May substitute glacéed fruit for dried fruit. Yield: 1½ pounds.

Jane Hereford, Illinois

Chocolate Peanut Clusters

6 ounces chocolate chips
2/3 cup sweetened condensed
  milk

1½ cups salted Spanish peanuts
1 teaspoon vanilla extract

Melt chocolate chips in double boiler over hot water, stirring until smooth. Remove from heat. Stir in condensed milk, peanuts, and vanilla. Drop by teaspoonfuls onto waxed paper. Let stand for several hours or until firm. Store in airtight container. Yield: 1½ dozen.

Paulette Armstrong, New Hampshire

Fantastic Fudge

2½ cups sugar
3/4 cup butter or margarine
2/3 cup evaporated milk
1/2 teaspoon salt
1½ cups creamy peanut butter
1 teaspoon vanilla extract

1 (7-ounce) jar marshmallow
  creme
1½ cups "M&M's" Plain
  Chocolate candies
3/4 cup chopped red candied
  cherries

Combine sugar, butter, milk and salt in heavy 3-quart saucepan. Bring to a full rolling boil over high heat, stirring constantly. Remove from heat. Stir in peanut butter until melted. Add vanilla and marshmallow creme; beat until blended. Fold in candies and cherries. Spread in buttered 9x13-inch dish. Let stand until cooled to room temperature. Cut into squares. Yield: 3 pounds.

Katie Carmicheal, South Dakota

Apricot Fudge

2/3 cup whipping cream
1/4 cup light corn syrup
1 (16-ounce) package
  confectioners' sugar
1/4 teaspoon salt
1/2 cup marshmallow creme

3 tablespoons butter or
  margarine
1/2 cup dried apricots, chopped
1 teaspoon vanilla extract
1 cup chopped walnuts

Combine cream, corn syrup, confectioners' sugar and salt in heavy 2-quart saucepan. Cook over low heat until sugar is completely dissolved, stirring constantly. Cook, covered, over medium heat for 2 to 3 minutes or until steam washes sugar crystals from side of pan. Cook, uncovered, over medium heat to 234 to 240 degrees on candy thermometer, soft-ball stage, stirring constantly. Add marshmallow creme, butter and apricots. Do not stir. Let stand for 15 minutes. Add vanilla and walnuts. Beat until creamy. Spoon into 8x8-inch dish. Chill in refrigerator. Cut into squares. Yield: 1 1/2 pounds.

Ann Neale, Texas

Pinwheels

2 1/2 cups sugar
1/2 cup light corn syrup
1/2 cup water
1/4 teaspoon salt
2 egg whites
1/2 teaspoon almond extract

Confectioners' sugar
1 cup finely chopped toasted
  almonds
1 cup finely chopped mixed red
  and green candied cherries

Combine sugar, corn syrup, water and salt in 2-quart saucepan. Bring to a boil over low heat; stir until sugar dissolves. Cook, covered, over high heat for 2 minutes or until steam dissolves sugar crystals from side of pan. Cook over medium heat to 260 degrees on candy thermometer, hard-ball stage; do not stir. Beat egg whites in large mixer bowl until stiff peaks form. Add hot syrup in a fine stream; beat constantly at high speed. Add almond flavoring. Beat for 4 minutes or until very stiff. Place on tea towel dusted generously with confectioners' sugar. Roll as thin as possible. Cut into strips about 4 inches wide. Sprinkle with mixture of almonds and candied cherries; press in lightly. Roll each strip tightly as for jelly roll from long side. Rolls should not be more than 1 inch in diameter. Wrap individually in foil. Store in refrigerator. Cut into thin slices. Yield: 2 pounds.

Myra Brown, Oklahoma

Impossible Cheese Fudge

1 cup butter or margarine
8 ounces Velveeta cheese
1/2 cup unsweetened baking
   cocoa

2 (16-ounce) packages
   confectioners' sugar
1 1/2 teaspoons vanilla extract
1 cup chopped pecans

Combine butter and cheese in double boiler pan. Cook over hot water until melted. Sift cocoa and confectioners' sugar into large bowl. Add cheese mixture and vanilla; mix quickly. Spread in buttered 9x13-inch dish. Sprinkle pecans on top. Let stand until firm. Cut into squares or diamonds. Yield: 3 pounds.

Hope Diamond, Alabama

Peanut Butter and Apple Fudge

6 ounces semisweet chocolate
   chips
5 ounces marshmallow creme
1 teaspoon vanilla extract

1/2 cup creamy peanut butter
2 cups sugar
2/3 cup apple juice

Combine chocolate chips, marshmallow creme, vanilla and peanut butter in large bowl. Combine sugar and apple juice in saucepan. Cook over medium heat until sugar dissolves and mixture comes to a boil, stirring constantly. Cook to 140 degrees on candy thermometer, soft-ball stage, stirring constantly. Pour over chocolate chip mixture. Stir until ingredients are blended. Pour into buttered 9x9-inch dish. Let stand until cool. Cut into squares. Yield: 2 pounds.

Marilyn Milner, New York

Crystal Candy

2 cups sugar
1/2 cup light corn syrup
1/8 teaspoon salt

1/2 cup water
Red or green food coloring
4 to 6 drops of oil of cinnamon

Cook first 3 ingredients and 1/2 cup water in heavy saucepan to 290 degrees on candy thermometer. Stir in food coloring and flavoring. Drop by teaspoonfuls onto cookie sheet. May substitute oil of peppermint or wintergreen for oil of cinnamon. Yield: 1 1/2 pounds.

Donis Ruth Eisiminger, Missouri

Halloween Haystacks

3 ounces cream cheese, softened
1/4 cup milk
4 cups confectioners' sugar
4 ounces chocolate, melted

1/2 teaspoon vanilla extract
1/8 teaspoon salt
6 cups miniature marshmallows
7 ounces flaked coconut

Blend cream cheese and milk in bowl. Mix in confectioners' sugar gradually. Stir in chocolate, vanilla and salt. Fold in marshmallows. Drop by heaping spoonfuls into coconut; toss to coat. Place on waxed paper-lined plate. Chill for 1 hour or until firm. Yield: 35 servings.

Drenda Bland, New Jersey

Holiday Wreaths

1/2 cup butter or margarine
1   (10-ounce) package
   marshmallows

1 teaspoon green food coloring
6 cups cornflakes
Red cinnamon candies

Melt butter in large saucepan over low heat. Add marshmallows. Cook until marshmallows melt and mixture is syrupy, stirring constantly. Remove from heat. Add food coloring; blend well. Add cornflakes; stir until coated. Divide into 1/4 cup portions. Shape mixture into 3-inch wreaths with buttered fingers. Decorate with cinnamon candies. Let stand until cool. Yield: Fourteen 3-inch wreaths.

Sallie Mason, Utah

Lollipops

3/4 cup sugar
1/2 cup light corn syrup
1/4 cup butter or margarine

Red food coloring
1 drop of oil of cinnamon
12 wooden skewers

Butter heavy 2-quart saucepan. Add sugar, corn syrup and butter. Cook over medium heat until sugar dissolves and mixture comes to a boil, stirring constantly. Cook to 270 degrees on candy thermometer, soft-crack stage. Remove from heat. Let stand for 5 minutes. Stir in food coloring and flavoring. Place skewers 4 inches apart on foil-lined surface. Spoon a small amount of candy syrup over top end of each skewer to cover. Drizzle remaining candy syrup from tip of tablespoon over skewers to form 3-inch lollipops. Let stand until lollipops are firm. Peel foil from lollipops. Wrap individually in plastic wrap. Yield: 1 dozen.

Sharon Lucas, Iowa

Peanut Butter Cups

3/4 cup butter or margarine,
  softened
2 1/2 to 3 cups confectioners'
  sugar

1 1/2 cups peanut butter
1 pound white almond bark
2 (8-ounce) milk chocolate
  candy bars

Cream butter, confectioners' sugar and peanut butter in bowl until light and fluffy. Chill for several hours. Melt almond bark and candy bars in double boiler; mix well. Shape peanut butter mixture into balls; flatten slightly. Spoon 1 tablespoon chocolate mixture into paper-lined miniature muffin cups. Place 1 peanut butter ball in each. Top with 1 tablespoon chocolate. Chill until firm. Yield: 4 dozen.

Jody Lorash, Montana

Peanut Butter Pinwheels

4 1/2 cups sugar
1 (12-ounce) can evaporated
  milk
1 (7-ounce) jar marshmallow
  creme
1/4 cup butter or margarine

2 cups peanut butter chips
1/4 cup melted butter or
  margarine
1/2 cup unsweetened baking
  cocoa
1 teaspoon vanilla extract

Combine sugar, evaporated milk, marshmallow creme and 1/4 cup butter in 4-quart saucepan. Bring to a boil over medium heat, stirring constantly. Cook for 5 minutes, stirring constantly. Combine half the hot mixture with 1 cup peanut butter chips in bowl. Stir until peanut butter chips melt. Spread in foil-lined 9x13-inch dish. Combine remaining hot mixture with 1 cup peanut butter chips, 1/4 cup melted butter, cocoa and vanilla in bowl. Beat until peanut butter chips melt and mixture is thickened. Spread over peanut butter layer. Let stand until firm. Invert onto foil-lined surface. Roll as for jelly roll from long side. Let stand until firm. Cut into slices. Store in airtight container. Yield: 4 pounds.

Vera Styles, Michigan

♥ *Save coffee cans and cover them with bright contact paper. Use them as airtight containers for packaging and delivering candy gifts.*

Pralines

1 cup sugar
1 cup packed light brown sugar
1/2 cup evaporated milk
1/8 teaspoon salt
2 cups pecan halves

2 tablespoons butter or
  margarine
2 teaspoons vanilla extract
3 tablespoons Kahlua

Combine sugars, evaporated milk and salt in heavy 2-quart saucepan. Cook over low heat until sugar dissolves, stirring constantly. Bring mixture to a full rolling boil over medium heat. Cook to 234 degrees on candy thermometer, soft-ball stage. Remove from heat. Stir in pecans, butter, vanilla and Kahlua. Cook over medium heat to 234 degrees, soft-ball stage. Drop by tablespoonfuls onto foil. Cool. Remove from foil. Stack between layers of waxed paper in loosely covered container. Yield: 2 dozen.

Della Davis, Utah

California Pralines

2 cups sugar
1 cup packed light brown sugar

1 cup half and half
1 cup chopped pistachios

Combine sugar, brown sugar and half and half in heavy 3-quart saucepan. Cook over low heat until sugars dissolve, stirring constantly. Bring to a boil over medium heat. Cook to 236 degrees on candy thermometer, soft-ball stage, stirring frequently. Remove from heat. Add pistachios; stir just until pistachios are coated. Drop by spoonfuls into 3-inch patties on buttered baking sheet. Add 1 or 2 drops of hot water if candy becomes too stiff to drop. Let stand until firm. Yield: 20 pralines.

Martha DeWhitt, Kansas

Rocky Road Clusters

16 ounces milk chocolate
3 cups miniature marshmallows
1 cup coarsely chopped pecans

1/2 cup miniature chocolate
  chips

Melt milk chocolate in double boiler over hot water. Remove from heat. Add marshmallows, pecans and chocolate chips; stir until coated. Drop by spoonfuls onto waxed paper. Let stand until firm. Store in cool place. Yield: 2 pounds.

Eliza Benton, Oregon

Peppermint Crunchies

1/2 cup evaporated milk
1/2 cup sugar
1 tablespoon light corn syrup
1 cup semisweet chocolate chips

1/2 cup coarsely chopped
   peppermint stick candy
1 cup chopped nuts
1/4 teaspoon peppermint extract

Mix evaporated milk, sugar and corn syrup in saucepan. Bring to a boil, stirring constantly. Cook for 2 minutes, stirring constantly. Remove from heat. Add chocolate chips; stir until chocolate is melted. Cool for 10 minutes. Stir in peppermint candy, nuts and flavoring. Drop by teaspoonfuls onto waxed paper-lined surface. Let stand until firm. Yield: 2 dozen.

Samantha Wood, Louisiana

Rocky Road Halloween Squares

1 (12-ounce) package chocolate
   chips
1 can sweetened condensed
   milk

2 tablespoons butter
2 cups dry-roasted peanuts
1 (10 1/2-ounce) package
   miniature marshmallows

Melt chocolate chips in condensed milk and butter in double boiler. Remove from heat. Mix peanuts and marshmallows; fold into chocolate mixture. Spread in waxed paper-lined 9x13-inch pan. Chill for 2 hours or until firm; remove from pan. Peel off waxed paper; cut into squares. Store, covered, at room temperature. Yield: 40 servings.

Micki McCorkle, Montana

Spooky Spiders

1 cup chocolate chips
1 cup butterscotch chips
1 (4-ounce) package salted
   peanuts

1 (3-ounce) can chow mein
   noodles
Silver candy shot

Melt chocolate and butterscotch chips over low heat, stirring constantly. Stir in peanuts and noodles. Drop by spoonfuls onto waxed paper. Add silver candy shot for eyes. Yield: 2 to 3 dozen.

Paula Heck, Missouri

Microwave Almond Toffee

³/₄ cup butter or margarine
1 cup packed light brown sugar
¹/₂ cup finely chopped almonds

¹/₂ cup semisweet chocolate
  chips
¹/₄ cup finely chopped almonds

Microwave butter and brown sugar in glass bowl on High for 1 minute; beat until smooth. Microwave for 4 minutes longer. Stir in ¹/₂ cup almonds. Microwave for 2 minutes or until thick. Beat with wire whisk. Pour into 8x8-inch dish lined with buttered foil. Sprinkle chocolate chips over top. Let stand, covered with plastic wrap, for 4 minutes. Spread melted chocolate over top. Sprinkle with ¹/₄ cup almonds. Chill until chocolate is firm. Peel off foil. Break into pieces. Store, tightly covered, in refrigerator. Yield: 1 pound.

Vonita Tast, California

Chocolate Truffles

¹/₂ cup whipping cream
¹/₂ cup sugar
6 tablespoons butter or
  margarine
1 teaspoon vanilla extract

2 cups semisweet chocolate
  chips
¹/₂ cup unsweetened baking
  cocoa

Combine cream, sugar and butter in saucepan. Bring to a boil; remove from heat. Stir in vanilla. Add chocolate chips; stir until chocolate melts. Cool to room temperature, stirring occasionally. Chill, covered, for 12 hours or longer. Mixture will be soft. Drop by teaspoonfuls into cocoa; shape into balls. Place in paper bonbon cups. Store, tightly covered, in refrigerator. Yield: 1¹/₂ dozen.

Rachel Richmond, Massachusetts

White Christmas Candy

12 ounces white chocolate
2 cups salted peanuts

1¹/₂ cups broken thin pretzel
  sticks

Melt chocolate in double boiler over simmering water, stirring constantly. Cool for 5 minutes. Add peanuts and pretzels; mix gently until coated. Drop by rounded teaspoonfuls onto foil. Let stand until cool. Store candies in refrigerator. Yield: 3 dozen.

Harriet Beach, Georgia

♥ *Cookie Gifts* ♥

White Almond Bars

2 cups all-purpose flour
1 cup melted butter or
  margarine
4 eggs
2 cups sugar

¹/₄ teaspoon salt
2 teaspoons almond flavoring
¹/₄ cup sugar
1 cup slivered almonds

Preheat oven to 325 degrees. Mix flour and butter in bowl; set aside. Beat eggs, 2 cups sugar and salt in mixer bowl until thick and lemon-colored. Add flour mixture and flavoring; mix well. Pour into greased and floured 9x13-inch baking pan. Sprinkle with remaining ¹/₄ cup sugar and almonds. Bake for 30 minutes. Cool in pan. Cut into bars. Yield: 3 dozen.

Jane Belmont, California

Bewitched Monster Cookies

6 eggs
1 (16-ounce) box light brown
   sugar
2 cups sugar
1¹/₂ teaspoons vanilla extract
1¹/₂ teaspoons corn syrup
4 teaspoons soda
1 (24-ounce) jar peanut butter

¹/₂ pound butter or margarine,
   softened
9 cups oats
1 (6-ounce) package chocolate
   chips
1 (8-ounce) package "M&M's"
   Plain Chocolate Candies

Preheat oven to 350 degrees. Mix first 8 ingredients until smooth. Stir in oats, chocolate chips and candies. Drop by ice cream scoopfuls onto greased cookie sheet. Bake for 12 minutes. Yield: 9 dozen.

Debbie Winkler, Illinois

♥ *Use red and green "M&M" Plain Chocolate Candies to transform Monster cookies into Christmas cookies.*

Apricot and Coconut Balls

1 cup dried apricots	2 tablespoons apricot Brandy
1/2 cup evaporated milk	2 cups fine graham cracker
3 cups flaked coconut	crumbs
1 cup confectioners' sugar	

Chop apricots. Combine with evaporated milk, coconut, confectioners' sugar and Brandy in bowl; mix well. Shape into 3/4-inch balls; roll in cracker crumbs. Store, wrapped, in refrigerator or freezer. Yield: 5 dozen.

Morgan Liane Jones, Tennessee

Bunny Carrot Bars

4 eggs, beaten	1 1/4 teaspoons cinnamon
2 cups sugar	6 ounces cream cheese, softened
1 1/4 cups vegetable oil	2 1/2 cups confectioners' sugar
2 (7 1/2-ounce) jars strained	1/2 cup butter or margarine,
carrots	softened
2 cups all-purpose flour	2 teaspoons vanilla extract
2 teaspoons soda	Jelly beans

Preheat oven to 350 degrees. Mix eggs, sugar, oil and carrots in bowl. Stir in dry ingredients. Spoon batter into greased and floured baking pans. Bake for 25 minutes. Blend cream cheese, confectioners' sugar, butter and vanilla in bowl until smooth. Spread over cooled cakes. Garnish with jelly beans.

I. Marie Gilman, Iowa

Chocolate Chip Brownies

1 (20-ounce) roll chocolate chip	1 cup sugar
refrigerator cookie dough	24 ounces cream cheese,
3 eggs	softened

Preheat oven to 375 degrees. Cut cookie dough roll into halves lengthwise. Cut each half into slices. Place half the slices in bottom of greased and floured 9x13-inch baking pan. Cookies may not cover bottom. Beat eggs, sugar and cream cheese in bowl until smooth. Pour over sliced cookie dough. Top with remaining cookie dough. Slices will not overlap. Bake for 40 to 45 minutes or until golden brown. Cut into squares. Yield: 5 dozen.

Anna Lawrence, Arkansas

Blarney Stones

2 cups sugar
4 egg yolks
2 cups all-purpose flour
4 teaspoons baking powder
1 cup boiling water
4 egg whites
1 teaspoon vanilla extract
Melted butter or margarine

Half and half
2 (16-ounce) boxes
confectioners' sugar
Several drops of green food
coloring
2 1/2 to 3 packages crushed
peanuts

Preheat oven to 325 degrees. Cream sugar and egg yolks until fluffy. Beat in flour and baking powder alternately with boiling water. Fold in stiffly beaten egg whites and vanilla. Bake in 9x13-inch baking pan for 45 minutes; cool. Cut into 1 1/2-inch squares. Mix enough melted butter and half and half with confectioners' sugar to make of spreading consistency. Stir in food coloring. Frost squares on all sides. Roll in peanuts. Yield: 3 1/3 dozen.

Vera V. Spencer, Kansas

Minty Glazed Brownies

2 ounces unsweetened chocolate
1/2 cup butter
2 eggs
1 cup sugar
1 teaspoon vanilla extract
1/2 cup all-purpose flour
1/4 teaspoon salt
1/2 cup chopped nuts

1/2 cup butter, softened
3 cups confectioners' sugar
5 tablespoons cream
1/2 teaspoon peppermint extract
1/2 ounce unsweetened
chocolate
1/2 teaspoon butter

Preheat oven to 350 degrees. Melt 2 ounces chocolate with 1/2 cup butter in double boiler over hot water. Beat eggs in mixer bowl until light. Add sugar gradually, beating constantly. Blend in chocolate and vanilla. Add mixture of flour and salt; mix well. Stir in nuts. Spread in greased 8x8-inch baking pan. Bake for 20 minutes or just until brownies begin to pull from sides of pan. Cool in pan. Cream 1/2 cup butter and confectioners' sugar in mixer bowl until light and fluffy. Add cream and flavoring. Spread over brownies. Chill until firm. Melt 1/2 ounce chocolate and 1/2 teaspoon butter in double boiler over hot water. Drizzle over brownies. Chill until set. Cut into squares. Yield: 20 brownies.

Donna Tignor, Texas

Chocolate and Cherry Drops

1¼ cups butter or margarine,
  softened
2 cups sugar
2 eggs
2 teaspoons vanilla extract
2½ cups all-purpose flour
¾ cup cocoa

1 teaspoon soda
1 teaspoon salt
2 cups chopped maraschino
  cherries, drained
1 cup chopped nuts
36 whole maraschino cherries

Preheat oven to 350 degrees. Cream butter and sugar in mixer bowl until light and fluffy. Add eggs and vanilla; mix well. Stir in mixture of flour, cocoa, soda and salt. Fold in chopped cherries and nuts. Chill, covered, in refrigerator for 30 minutes. Drop by teaspoonfuls onto ungreased cookie sheet. Cut cherries into halves. Place one cherry half on each cookie. Bake for 10 minutes or until crisp around edges. Remove to wire rack to cool. Yield: 6 dozen.

Mary Rodgers, Alabama

Chocolate Chip Drops

¼ cup butter or margarine,
  softened
3 ounces cream cheese, softened
½ cup sugar
¼ cup packed light brown
  sugar
1 egg
½ teaspoon vanilla extract

1⅓ cups all-purpose flour
¼ teaspoon soda
½ teaspoon salt
1 cup semisweet chocolate chips
½ cup chopped nuts
¼ cup drained chopped
  maraschino cherries
36 candied red cherry halves

Preheat oven to 375 degrees. Cream butter, cream cheese, sugar, brown sugar, egg and vanilla in mixer bowl until light and fluffy. Combine flour, soda and salt in small bowl. Add to creamed mixture; mix well. Stir in chocolate chips, nuts and chopped cherries. Drop by rounded teaspoonfuls onto ungreased cookie sheet. Top each cookie with cherry half. Bake for 8 minutes or just until set. Remove immediately to wire rack to cool. Yield: 3 dozen.

Sue Henson, Kentucky

Chocolate-Covered Raisin Cookies

1 cup butter or margarine, softened	2 eggs
3/4 cup sugar	1 teaspoon vanilla extract
3/4 cup packed light brown sugar	2 1/4 cups all-purpose flour
	1 teaspoon soda
	2 cups chocolate-covered raisins

Preheat oven to 375 degrees. Cream butter, sugar and brown sugar in mixer bowl until light and fluffy. Blend in eggs and vanilla. Mix flour and soda in bowl. Add to creamed mixture gradually, mixing well after each addition. Stir in chocolate-covered raisins. Drop by rounded teaspoonfuls onto cookie sheet. Bake for 8 to 10 minutes. Cool on cookie sheet for several minutes. Cool on wire rack. Yield: 4 dozen.

Geno Rodgers, Michigan

Chocolate Finger Cookies

2/3 cup butter or margarine, softened	1/2 cup unsweetened baking cocoa
1 cup sugar	1/2 teaspoon soda
2 eggs	1/4 teaspoon salt
2 teaspoons vanilla extract	Chocolate Glaze
2 1/2 cups unsifted all-purpose flour	3/4 cup chopped pecans
	30 candied cherry halves

Preheat oven to 350 degrees. Cream butter and sugar in bowl until light and fluffy. Add eggs and vanilla; mix well. Mix flour, cocoa, soda and salt. Add to creamed mixture; mix well. Shape by heaping teaspoonfuls into 3-inch fingers; place on ungreased cookie sheet. Bake for 8 to 10 minutes or until set but not hard. Cool on cookie sheet for 1 to 2 minutes. Remove to wire rack to cool completely. Spread with Chocolate Glaze. Sprinkle with pecans; top with cherry half. Yield: 2 1/2 dozen.

Chocolate Glaze

2 tablespoons butter	3 tablespoons unsweetened baking cocoa
2 tablespoons water	1/2 teaspoon vanilla extract
1 cup confectioners' sugar	

Bring butter and water to a boil in saucepan. Remove from heat. Stir in confectioners' sugar, cocoa and vanilla; beat until smooth.

Nancy Barkley, Idaho

Chocolate Peanut Butter Chip Cookies

1 cup butter or margarine,
  softened
2 cups sugar
2 teaspoons vanilla extract
2 eggs
1/4 cup milk

3 cups all-purpose flour
2/3 cup unsweetened baking
  cocoa
1 teaspoon soda
2 cups peanut butter chips

Preheat oven to 350 degrees. Cream butter, sugar and vanilla in bowl until light and fluffy. Add eggs and milk; beat until blended. Mix flour, cocoa and soda. Add to creamed mixture; mix well. Stir in peanut butter chips. Drop by teaspoonfuls onto ungreased cookie sheet. Bake for 8 to 10 minutes. Cool on cookie sheet for 1 to 2 minutes. Remove to wire rack to cool completely. Yield: 7 dozen.

Lulu Watkins, Louisiana

Peanutty Brownie Bars

3/4 cup melted butter
1/2 cup unsweetened
  baking cocoa
1 1/2 cups sugar
1 1/2 teaspoons vanilla extract
3 eggs
1 1/4 cups all-purpose flour

1/2 cup sugar
1/2 cup water
2 cups peanut butter chips
1/2 cup semisweet chocolate
  chips
1 tablespoon shortening
1/4 teaspoon vanilla extract

Preheat oven to 350 degrees. Line 10x15-inch baking pan with greased foil. Combine butter and cocoa in bowl; mix well. Add 1 1/2 cups sugar and 1 1/2 teaspoons vanilla; mix well. Add eggs 1 at a time, beating well after each addition. Stir in flour. Spread in prepared pan. Bake for 12 minutes. Cool for 2 minutes. Invert onto wire rack; peel off foil. Cool completely. Combine 1/2 cup sugar and water in saucepan. Bring to a boil; remove from heat. Add peanut butter chips; stir until chips melt. Cool slightly. Cut baked layer into two 7 1/2x10-inch layers. Spread peanut butter mixture between and on top of layers. Combine chocolate chips and shortening in double boiler. Heat over hot water until melted. Stir in 1/4 teaspoon vanilla. Drizzle over brownie layers. Let stand until set. Cut into bars. Yield: 3 dozen.

Lisa Gaither, Kansas

Chocolate Teddy Bears

2/3 cup butter or margarine,
  softened
1 cup sugar
2 teaspoons vanilla extract
2 eggs

2 1/2 cups all-purpose flour
1/2 cup unsweetened baking
  cocoa
1/2 teaspoon soda
1/4 teaspoon salt

Cream butter, sugar and vanilla in mixer bowl until light and fluffy. Blend in eggs. Combine flour, cocoa, soda and salt in bowl. Add to creamed mixture gradually, mixing well after each addition. Chill until firm enough to handle easily. Preheat oven to 350 degrees. Shape 1 to 1 1/2-inch ball of dough for body of bear. Place on ungreased cookie sheet, pressing to flatten slightly. Shape 3/4 to 1-inch ball of dough for head. Attach to body by overlapping slightly and pressing gently. Shape four 1/2-inch balls for legs, 2 smaller balls for ears and a tiny ball for nose. Attach to body and head. Draw eyes, mouth, buttons and paws with wooden pick. Pierce small hole at top of cookie for ribbon if cookie is to be used as ornament. Repeat process with remaining dough. Bake for 6 to 8 minutes or until set. Cool on cookie sheet for 1 minute; remove to wire rack to cool completely. Store in covered container. Dry cookies to be used as ornaments on wire rack for 6 hours or longer. Pull ribbons through holes at top of cookies for hanging. Tie additional ribbons around necks of bears. Yield: 1 dozen.

Martha Brown, Montana

Chocolate Thin Mint Cookies

1/2 cup butter or margarine,
  softened
3/4 cup sugar
1 egg
1 teaspoon vanilla extract
1 1/2 cups all-purpose flour

1/4 cup unsweetened
  baking cocoa
1/2 teaspoon soda
1/4 teaspoon salt
1 (6-ounce) package junior
  mints

Cream butter and sugar in mixer bowl until light and fluffy. Blend in egg and vanilla. Sift flour, cocoa, soda and salt together. Add to creamed mixture gradually, mixing at low speed after each addition. Chill for 30 minutes. Preheat oven to 350 degrees. Shape by teaspoonfuls into 1 1/2-inch balls. Place 2 1/2 inches apart on greased cookie sheet. Press mint into center of each ball, shaping dough up and around edge of mint. Bake for 8 to 10 minutes or just until set. Cool on cookie sheet for 5 minutes. Remove to wire rack to cool completely. Yield: 2 dozen.

Shirley Joiner, Florida

Filled Chocolate Bars

1/2 cup butter or margarine
2 ounces unsweetened baking
  chocolate
2 eggs, beaten
1 cup sugar
1/2 cup all-purpose flour

1/4 teaspoon salt
1 teaspoon vanilla extract
1 cup finely chopped almonds
Chocolate Filling
Easy Chocolate Glaze
1/2 cup sliced almonds

Preheat oven to 400 degrees. Melt butter in saucepan; remove from heat. Add baking chocolate; stir until melted. Combine eggs, sugar, flour and salt in bowl; beat until blended. Add melted chocolate and vanilla; mix well. Stir in chopped almonds. Pour into greased and waxed paper-lined 10x15-inch baking pan. Bake for 10 minutes. Cool. Cut into halves crosswise. Invert onto cutting board. Spread Chocolate Filling over 1 cookie layer; top with remaining cookie layer. Spread with Chocolate Glaze. Garnish with sliced almonds. Cut into bars. Yield: 2 dozen.

Chocolate Filling

1 cup confectioners' sugar
1 tablespoon milk
1/2 teaspoon vanilla extract

2 tablespoons butter or
  margarine, softened

Combine confectioners' sugar, milk, vanilla and butter in small bowl; beat until smooth. Yield: 1/4 cup.

Easy Chocolate Glaze

1/4 cup sugar
2 tablespoons water

1/2 cup semisweet chocolate
  chips

Bring sugar dissolved in water to a boil in small saucepan; remove from heat. Add chocolate chips; stir until melted. Yield: 1/4 cup.

Jessica Smithson, Utah

Double Dutch Cookies

3/4 cup butter or margarine,
  softened
1 cup sugar
1 egg
1 teaspoon vanilla extract
1 1/2 cups all-purpose flour
1/4 cup unsweetened baking
  cocoa

1/2 teaspoon soda
1/4 teaspoon salt
1/2 cup "M&M's" Plain
  Chocolate Candies
1/2 cup chopped pecans
1/2 cup raisins
100 "M&M's" Plain Chocolate
  Candies

Preheat oven to 350 degrees. Cream butter and sugar in bowl until light and fluffy. Beat in egg and vanilla. Combine flour, cocoa, soda and salt. Add to creamed mixture; mix well. Stir in 1/2 cup candies, pecans and raisins. Drop dough by heaping tablespoonfuls onto greased cookie sheet. Press 4 candies into each cookie. Bake for 8 to 10 minutes or until edges are set. Cool on cookie sheet for 2 to 3 minutes. Remove to wire rack to cool completely. Yield: 2 dozen.

Ann Stevens, Iowa

Cinnamon Sledges

1 cup butter or margarine,
  softened
1/2 cup packed light brown
  sugar
1/2 cup sugar
1 egg yolk

2 cups all-purpose flour
1 tablespoon cinnamon
1/8 teaspoon salt
1 egg white
1 1/2 cups chopped pecans

Preheat oven to 300 degrees. Cream butter, brown sugar, sugar and egg yolk in large mixer bowl at medium speed until light and fluffy. Add mixture of flour, cinnamon and salt. Beat just until blended. Dough will be stiff. Spread evenly in 10x15-inch pan. Beat egg white in mixer bowl just until foamy. Spread evenly on top of dough. Press pecans lightly on top. Bake for 35 to 40 minutes or until golden brown. Cut into bars while hot. Yield: 3 dozen.

Florence Milner, South Carolina

Cinnamon Snowballs

1 cup butter or margarine,
  softened
1/3 cup sugar
2 teaspoons vanilla extract
3/4 cup cornflake crumbs

1 3/4 cups all-purpose flour
1 teaspoon cinnamon
1 cup finely chopped nuts
2 cups (or more) sifted
  confectioners' sugar

Preheat oven to 350 degrees. Cream butter and sugar in mixer bowl until light and fluffy. Add vanilla. Add crumbs, flour, cinnamon and nuts; mix well. Shape into 3/4-inch balls. Place on ungreased cookie sheet. Bake for 15 minutes or until light brown. Place confectioners' sugar in brown paper bag. Add warm cookies; shake gently. Cool on wire rack. Roll in additional confectioners' sugar. Yield: 7 dozen.

Brenda Sordelett, Virginia

Confetti Squares

4 eggs
2 cups packed light brown sugar
2/3 cup peanut butter
1/2 cup melted butter or
  margarine
1 teaspoon vanilla extract

2 cups all-purpose flour
1 teaspoon baking powder
1 teaspoon salt
1/4 teaspoon soda
1 1/2 cups chopped "M&M's"
  Plain Chocolate Candies

Preheat oven to 350 degrees. Beat eggs in mixer bowl at high speed for 2 minutes. Beat in brown sugar. Add peanut butter, butter and vanilla; blend well. Combine flour, baking powder, salt and soda. Add to peanut butter mixture; mix well. Stir in 1 cup candies. Spread batter in greased 10x15-inch baking pan. Sprinkle with remaining 1/2 cup candies. Bake for 25 to 28 minutes or until set; do not overbake. Cool completely. Cut into squares. Yield: 3 to 4 dozen.

Anna Lise Wiggens, Nevada

Holiday Florentines

1/2 cup butter or margarine
1/2 cup sugar
2 tablespoons honey
1/2 cup sliced almonds
1/3 cup chopped candied
  cherries

1/3 cup chopped candied
  orange peel
1 cup all-purpose flour, sifted
2/3 cup semisweet chocolate
  chips

Preheat oven to 350 degrees. Combine butter, sugar and honey in saucepan. Cook over low heat until butter melts. Remove from heat. Stir in almonds, cherries, orange peel and flour. Drop by heaping teaspoonfuls onto parchment-lined cookie sheet. Bake for 10 minutes. Cool on cookie sheet. Melt chocolate chips in double boiler pan over hot water. Turn cookies over. Spread chocolate on bottoms of cookies. Make wavy pattern in chocolate with fork. Let stand until chocolate is set. Yield: 1½ dozen.

Mary Horton, Mississippi

Shamrock Cookies

¼ cup butter, softened
1 (4-ounce) package pistachio instant pudding mix
1⅓ cups buttermilk baking mix

1 egg
1 tablespoon sugar
1 can vanilla frosting, tinted green

Preheat oven to 350 degrees. Cream butter and pudding mix in mixer bowl. Add baking mix, egg and sugar; mix well. Roll on lightly floured board to ⅜-inch thickness. Cut with shamrock-shaped cookie cutter. Bake on lightly greased cookie sheet for 9 to 10 minutes. Cool on wire racks. Top with frosting. Yield 1½ dozen.

Jane Cervantes, Ohio

Jack-O'-Lantern Tea Cakes

1 recipe sugar cookie dough
1½ cups confectioners' sugar
1 to 2 tablespoons milk
½ teaspoon orange extract
Several drops of green food coloring

Several drops of red and yellow food coloring
Candy corn
Shoestring licorice

Shape cookie dough into pumpkins with stems. Bake using recipe directions. Blend confectioners' sugar, milk and orange flavoring to spreading consistency. Tint 1 tablespoonful with green food coloring for stems. Tint remaining frosting with red and yellow food coloring blended to make orange. Frost cookies. Decorate with candy corn for eyes and nose and licorice for mouth. Yield: 2 dozen.

Edris Christians, Arkansas

Butter Kisses

1/2 cup butter, softened	1/4 teaspoon soda
1/2 cup sugar	11/4 cups all-purpose flour
1 egg	1/2 cup finely ground nuts
1 teaspoon vanilla extract	30 milk chocolate kisses

Preheat oven to 350 degrees. Cream butter, sugar, egg and vanilla in bowl until light and fluffy. Add mixture of soda and flour; mix well. Shape into 1-inch balls. Roll in nuts. Place on ungreased cookie sheet. Bake for 8 minutes or until almost set. Press chocolate kiss into center of each cookie. Bake for 2 minutes longer. Cool on wire rack. Yield: 3 dozen.

Cindy Garren, South Carolina

Ice Cream Cookies

2 cups butter or margarine, softened	1 pint vanilla ice cream
	Confectioners' sugar
4 cups all-purpose flour	1 (21-ounce) can fruit pie filling

Cut butter into flour in bowl until crumbly. Mix in ice cream. Chill overnight. Preheat oven to 350 degrees. Roll dough on surface sprinkled with 1/4 inch confectioners' sugar. Cut as desired. Make indentation in each cookie. Fill with fruit filling. Place on cookie sheet. Bake for 15 minutes. Cool on wire rack. Yield: 6 dozen.

Eva Courtney, Washington

Easy Cheesy Lemon Bars

1 (18-ounce) package lemon cake mix	1 egg
	8 ounces cream cheese, softened
1/2 cup butter or margarine, softened	1 (16-ounce) can lemon frosting
	2 eggs

Preheat oven to 350 degrees. Combine cake mix, butter and 1 egg in mixer bowl; mix well. Press into bottom of greased 9x13-inch baking pan. Blend cream cheese and frosting in mixer bowl. Reserve 1/2 cup for frosting. Add 2 eggs to remaining frosting mixture. Beat for 3 minutes. Spread over mixture in pan. Bake for 30 minutes or until golden. Cool. Spread frosting mixture over top. Cut into bars. Yield: 3 dozen.

Beverely Miller, Mississippi

Holiday Lime Bars

1 cup butter or margarine,
  softened
3/4 cup sugar
1 egg yolk
1 tablespoon grated lime rind

2 tablespoons fresh lime juice
2 cups all-purpose flour
1 egg white, beaten
1 cup flaked coconut
3/4 cup confectioners' sugar

Preheat oven to 350 degrees. Cream butter and sugar in mixer bowl until light and fluffy. Add egg yolk, lime rind and 1 tablespoon lime juice; mix well. Add flour; mix well. Spread in greased 10x15-inch baking pan. Brush with egg white. Sprinkle with coconut. Bake for 20 minutes or until golden. Cool. Blend confectioners' sugar and 1 tablespoon lime juice in bowl. Drizzle over baked layer. Cut into bars. Yield: 3 1/2 dozen.

Elizabeth Jenkins, New York

Macadamia Nut Cookies

1 cup butter or margarine,
  softened
1/2 cup confectioners' sugar
1/4 teaspoon almond extract

2 cups cake flour
1 cup finely chopped
  macadamia nuts
1/2 to 1 cup sugar

Cream butter and confectioners' sugar in mixer bowl until light and fluffy. Add almond extract; mix well. Add cake flour and macadamia nuts; mix well. Chill for several hours. Preheat oven to 325 degrees. Shape into balls on cookie sheet; flatten. Bake for 10 minutes. Roll hot cookies in sugar. Yield: 2 1/2 dozen.

Leslie Tignor, Alabama

Pine Nut Macaroons

1 pound almond paste
1 1/2 cups sugar
4 egg whites

1 1/2 cups chopped pine nuts
48 whole pine nuts

Preheat oven to 400 degrees. Combine almond paste and sugar in food processor container. Process until crumbly. Beat egg whites in mixer bowl until medium-stiff peaks form. Fold in almond paste mixture and chopped pine nuts. Drop by spoonfuls onto cookie sheets lined with baking parchment. Top with whole pine nut. Bake for 12 minutes. Cool on cookie sheets. Yield: 4 dozen.

Marian Sherman, California

Oatmeal Tea Wafers

1 egg white	1/2 cup sugar
1/2 cup corn oil	1 cup quick-cooking oats
1 teaspoon vanilla extract	1/2 cup sifted all-purpose flour

Preheat oven to 375 degrees. Combine egg white, corn oil, vanilla and sugar in mixer bowl. Beat at medium speed until thick. Add mixture of oats and flour gradually, beating constantly at low speed until well mixed. Drop by level teaspoonfuls 3 inches apart onto foil-lined cookie sheet. Spread into 1 1/2-inch circles with spatula. Bake for 8 minutes or until light brown. Cool on foil on wire rack. Store in airtight container. Yield: 4 dozen.

Melandie Henson, Nevada

Peanut Butter Stars

1 cup peanut butter	1 egg, beaten
1 cup sugar	18 chocolate stars

Preheat oven to 350 degrees. Combine peanut butter, sugar and egg in bowl; mix well. Shape into 1 1/2-inch balls. Place on cookie sheet. Press with buttered glass bottom to flatten. Bake for 10 minutes or until light brown. Press 1 chocolate star into top of each cookie. Remove to wire rack to cool. Yield: 1 1/2 dozen.

Claudia Benson, Oregon

Pecan Icebox Cookies

1/2 cup butter or margarine, softened	1 egg
	1 1/2 cups all-purpose flour
1 cup sugar	1/2 teaspoon baking powder
1 teaspoon vanilla extract	1/2 cup chopped pecans

Cream butter and sugar in bowl until light and fluffy. Add vanilla and egg; mix well. Add mixture of flour and baking powder; mix well. Mix in pecans. Shape into two 1 1/4-inch diameter rolls. Wrap in waxed paper or plastic wrap. Chill in refrigerator for up to 1 week. Preheat oven to 400 degrees. Slice cookie dough into 1/4-inch slices; arrange on greased cookie sheet. Bake for 6 to 7 minutes or until very slightly brown on edges. Cool on cookie sheet for 1 minute. Remove to wire rack to cool completely. Yield: 6 dozen.

Anastasia Dillard, Nebraska

Halloween Pumpkin Cookies

1½ cups butter or margarine,
  softened
2 cups packed light brown sugar
1 cup sugar
1 egg
1 teaspoon vanilla extract
4 cups all-purpose flour
2 cups oats

2 teaspoons soda
2 teaspoons cinnamon
1 teaspoon salt
1 (16-ounce) can pumpkin
1 cup chocolate chips
1 tube chocolate decorator
  frosting

Preheat oven to 350 degrees. Beat butter and sugars until fluffy. Stir in egg and vanilla. Add mixture of next 5 dry ingredients alternately with pumpkin. Stir in chocolate chips. Drop by ¼ cupfuls onto greased cookie sheet. Shape dough to resemble pumpkins with stems. Bake for 20 to 25 minutes. Decorate with frosting to make jack-o'-lantern face.
Yield: 2½ to 3 dozen.

Sandra Nelson, Ohio

Ribbon Butter Cookies

1 cup butter or margarine,
  softened
1½ cups sugar
1 egg
1 teaspoon vanilla extract
2¼ cups all-purpose flour

1¼ teaspoons baking powder
¼ teaspoon salt
1 (1-ounce) square baking
  chocolate, melted
¼ cup chopped walnuts
2 drops of red food coloring

Cream butter and sugar in mixer bowl until light and fluffy. Beat in egg and vanilla. Add flour, baking powder and salt; mix well. Divide dough into 3 portions. Press 1 portion into 5x9-inch loaf pan lined with aluminum foil. Mix chocolate and walnuts into second portion. Press over plain layer. Mix food coloring into third portion. Press over top. Fold waxed paper over top of layers and press down evenly. Chill for 2 hours or longer. Preheat oven to 350 degrees. Set pan with dough into warm water for several minutes to loosen. Invert dough onto work surface; remove foil. Cut loaf into thirds lengthwise. Slice ¼ inch thick. Place 1 inch apart on ungreased cookie sheet. Bake for 10 minutes or until light brown. Remove to wire rack to cool. Yield: 5 dozen.

Mary Beth Lacey, North Carolina

Sesame Cookies

2 cups margarine, softened
1¼ cups sugar
3 cups all-purpose flour

1 cup sesame seed
2 cups shredded coconut
½ cup finely chopped almonds

Cream margarine and sugar in mixer bowl until light and fluffy. Add flour; mix well. Fold in sesame seed, coconut and almonds. Divide dough into 3 portions. Chill, covered, until firm. Preheat oven to 300 degrees. Shape dough into balls. Place on cookie sheet. Flatten with bottom of glass dipped in sugar. Bake for 30 minutes. Cool on wire rack. Yield: 4 dozen.

Carla Sanderson, New York

Sugar and Spice Snaps

¾ cup butter or margarine,
   softened
1 cup sugar
1 egg
¼ cup molasses

2 cups all-purpose flour
2 teaspoons soda
1 teaspoon cinnamon
½ teaspoon nutmeg
1 cup confectioners' sugar

Preheat oven to 350 degrees. Cream butter and sugar in bowl until light and fluffy. Add egg and molasses; mix well. Add mixture of flour, soda and spices; mix well. Chill, covered, for 1 hour. Shape into ¾-inch balls. Place 2 inches apart on greased cookie sheet. Bake for 8 minutes. Remove to wire rack; cool slightly. Sprinkle with confectioners' sugar. Yield: 6½ dozen.

Judy Chisenall, Illinois

Holly Wreaths

1 cup shortening
3 ounces cream cheese, softened
½ cup sugar

1 teaspoon vanilla extract
1 cup sifted all-purpose flour
2 drops of green food coloring

Preheat oven to 375 degrees. Cream shortening, cream cheese and sugar in mixer bowl until light and fluffy. Blend in vanilla. Add flour gradually. Tint with food coloring. Press through cookie press fitted with number-2 star plate into circles on ungreased cookie sheet. Bake for 8 minutes or until set. Cool on wire rack. Decorate with frosting leaves and red cinnamon candies if desired. Yield: 4 dozen.

Brook Adams, Florida

♥ *Potpourri Gifts* ♥

Golden Delicious Chutney

2 cups cider vinegar
2¼ cups sugar
4 cups chopped, peeled Golden
 Delicious apples
2 cloves of garlic, minced

³/4 cup chopped candied
 gingerroot
1 cup golden raisins
1 teaspoon white mustard seed
¹/2 teaspoon salt

Combine cider vinegar and sugar in heavy saucepan. Bring to a boil. Add apples, garlic, gingerroot, raisins, mustard seed and salt. Cook for 10 minutes or until apples are almost tender. Remove fruit with slotted spoon; reserve. Cook syrup over medium heat for 15 minutes or until thickened and reduced by half. Add fruit. Return to a boil. Spoon into hot sterilized jars, leaving ¹/2 inch headspace; seal with 2-piece lids. Process in boiling water bath for 10 minutes. Cool. Yield: 3 pints.

Gloria Whitworth, Mississippi

Tomato and Lime Chutney

4 cups chopped peeled tomatoes
1 large orange
2 medium limes

3 (2-inch) cinnamon sticks
1 tablespoon ginger
4 cups sugar

Drain tomatoes. Grate orange and lime rinds. Chop orange and lime pulp. Combine tomatoes, orange, limes, cinnamon sticks, ginger, grated rinds and sugar in large saucepan. Bring to a boil over medium heat; stir to dissolve sugar. Reduce heat. Simmer over low heat for 1 hour or until thick. Remove cinnamon sticks. Ladle into hot sterilized ¹/2-pint jars, leaving ¹/2 inch headspace; seal with 2-piece lids. Process in boiling water bath for 20 minutes. Yield: 2¹/2 pints.

Chelsea Reardon, Connecticut

Cranberry Chutney

1 pound fresh cranberries	1 firm pear, chopped
2 cups sugar	1 apple, chopped
1 cup water	1 tablespoon grated orange rind
1 envelope unflavored gelatin	2¹/2 teaspoons ginger
¹/4 cup water	1 cup golden raisins
1 cup orange juice	1 cup chopped pecans
1 cup chopped celery	

Combine cranberries, sugar and 1 cup water in saucepan. Bring to a boil over medium heat. Cook until sugar is dissolved, stirring constantly. Simmer for 15 minutes, stirring occasionally. Remove from heat. Soften gelatin in ¹/4 cup water. Stir into cranberry mixture until dissolved. Add orange juice, celery, pear, apple, orange rind, ginger and raisins; mix well. Chill, covered, for 3 hours. Stir in pecans. Spoon into serving dish. Yield: 8 servings.

Marilee Henson, Florida

Strawberry and Pineapple Jam

1 (10-ounce) package frozen strawberries in syrup, thawed	Grated rind and juice of 1 lemon
1 (20-ounce) can juice-pack crushed pineapple, drained	Grated rind and juice of 3 oranges
4¹/2 cups sugar	5 ounces liquid pectin

Combine strawberries and pineapple in deep heavy saucepan. Add sugar, grated fruit rinds and juices. Cook over medium heat until sugar dissolves, stirring frequently. Increase heat. Bring to a full rolling boil. Boil rapidly for 1 minute. Stir in liquid pectin. Boil for 4 to 5 minutes, stirring occasionally. Remove from heat. Stir for 5 minutes. Spoon into hot sterilized jars; seal. Store in freezer. Yield: 6 (7-ounce) jars.

Mary Beth Andrews, New Mexico

Cinnamon Candy Jelly

5¹/2 cups sugar	3 cups water
1 (6¹/2-ounce) package small cinnamon candies	1 (2-envelope) package Certo

Combine sugar, candies and water in saucepan. Let stand overnight. Cook over medium heat until sugar and candies are completely dissolved. Bring to a boil. Stir in Certo. Cook for 3 minutes, stirring constantly. Remove from heat. Let stand for several minutes. Skim foam from top. Pour into small sterilized jars, leaving 1/2 inch headspace; seal. Store in refrigerator. Yield: 8 (4-ounce) jars.

Shannon Hoosier, Arkansas

Jalapeño Jam

1 cup chopped green bell
  pepper
1 cup chopped jalapeño peppers
1 1/2 cups cider vinegar
6 cups sugar

1/2 teaspoon salt
1 teaspoon cayenne pepper
1/2 (6-ounce) bottle of pectin
Several drops of green food
  coloring

Combine green pepper, jalapeño peppers and cider vinegar 1/2 at a time in blender container. Purée until smooth. Combine purée, sugar, salt and cayenne pepper in saucepan. Bring to a boil. Cook for 2 minutes. Remove from heat. Add pectin. Let stand for 5 minutes, stirring constantly. Add food coloring; mix well. Pour into hot sterilized jars, leaving 1/2 inch headspace; seal. Store in refrigerator. Yield: 2 pints.

Alberta Cooper, Nebraska

Peach Butter

6 pounds fresh peaches
1/4 cup fresh lemon juice

1 teaspoon cinnamon
3 1/4 cups sugar

Peel peaches; cut into fourths. Purée in blender container. Combine 11 cups peach purée, lemon juice and cinnamon in large saucepan; mix well. Cook, uncovered, over medium heat for 2 hours, stirring frequently. Add sugar; mix well. Cook mixture, uncovered, until of desired consistency, stirring frequently. Ladle into hot sterilized jars, leaving 1/2 inch headspace; seal with 2-piece lids. Process in boiling water bath for 10 minutes. May substitute nectarines for peaches. Yield: 6 (8-ounce) jars.

Alexandria Phillips, Virginia

Holiday Fruit Butter

8 large Granny Smith apples
5 large Bartlett pears
1/2 cup water
2 bananas, sliced

4 cups sugar
1/3 cup fresh orange juice
1 teaspoon grated orange rind

Cut apples and pears into quarters. Combine with water in 5-quart saucepan. Cook over medium heat until fruit is tender, stirring occasionally. Add bananas. Put fruit through sieve. Add sugar, orange juice and orange rind; mix well. Cook over medium heat for 1 hour or until thick, stirring frequently. Pour into hot sterilized jars, leaving 1/2 inch headspace; seal with 2-piece lids. Process in boiling water bath for 10 minutes. Cool. Yield: 4 pints.

Doris Smithson, Pennsylvania

Orange-Apricot Conserve

1 pound dried apricots
1 large onion, chopped
1 orange, sectioned
2 cloves of garlic
5 slices crystallized ginger
2 1/2 cups cider vinegar

1 1/2 cups packed light brown
  sugar
1/2 cup golden raisins
1 teaspoon crushed red pepper
1 teaspoon salt
1   (3-inch) cinnamon stick

Mince apricots in food processor container fitted with metal blade. Place apricots in saucepan. Repeat process with onion, orange, garlic and ginger, mincing 1 at a time and adding each to apricots. Add vinegar, brown sugar, raisins, red pepper, salt and cinnamon stick; mix well. Bring to a boil over medium heat; reduce heat. Simmer over low heat for 45 minutes or until thickened; stir frequently. Remove cinnamon stick. Spoon mixture into hot sterilized 1/2-pint jars, leaving 1/2 inch headspace; seal with 2-piece lids. Store in refrigerator. Yield: 3 pints.

Susie Davidson, South Carolina

Pickled Asparagus

2 pounds fresh asparagus
4 sprigs of fresh dillweed
1/2 teaspoon cayenne pepper
2 cloves of garlic
2 1/2 cups white wine vinegar
1/4 cup salt
2 1/2 cups water
1/2 cup light corn syrup

Wash asparagus; drain. Trim spears to fit glass jars, removing tough portions of stalks. Pack asparagus spears vertically into hot sterilized jars, leaving 1 inch headspace. Place 2 sprigs of fresh dillweed between asparagus and side of jar. Add 1/4 teaspoon cayenne pepper and 1 clove of garlic to each jar. Combine wine vinegar, salt, water and corn syrup in saucepan. Bring to a boil. Pour into jars, leaving 1/2 inch headspace; seal. Refrigerate for several weeks. Rinse before serving. Yield: 2 quarts.

Annette Little, Rhode Island

Pickled Cauliflower

2 medium heads cauliflower
3/4 cup pickling salt
3 quarts cold water
1 1/2 cups sugar
3 1/2 cups white vinegar
1 cup water
1 tablespoon turmeric
2 tablespoons dry mustard
2 tablespoons onion powder
2 tablespoons mustard seed
1 tablespoon celery seed

Cut cauliflower into 2-inch pieces. Dissolve pickling salt in 3 quarts cold water in large crock. Add cauliflower. Let stand for 12 to 15 hours. Drain. Combine sugar, vinegar, water, turmeric, dry mustard, onion powder, mustard seed and celery seed in large saucepan. Cook over medium heat until sugar is dissolved. Add cauliflower, Cook for 10 minutes. Do not breathe vapor. Pack cauliflower into hot sterilized 1-pint jars. Add boiling liquid, leaving 1/2 inch headspace; seal with 2-piece lids. Store in refrigerator. Yield: 4 pints.

Abigail Reasonover, Wyoming

Red Cinnamon Pickles

2 gallons large cucumbers
2 cups pickling lime
8½ quarts water
1 cup vinegar
1 (1-ounce) bottle of red food
   coloring
1 tablespoon alum

2 cups vinegar
10 cups sugar
3 cups water
8 cinnamon sticks
1 (8-ounce) package red hot
   cinnamon candies

Peel and seed cucumbers; cut into sticks. Combine with lime and 8½ quarts water in large bowl. Let stand for 24 hours, stirring occasionally. Drain and rinse well. Cover with fresh water. Let stand for 3 hours. Drain. Combine cucumbers, 1 cup vinegar, food coloring and alum in saucepan. Add water to cover. Simmer for 2 hours. Drain. Combine 2 cups vinegar, sugar, 3 cups water, cinnamon sticks and candies in saucepan. Cook until candies dissolve. Pour over cucumbers. Let stand overnight. Drain into saucepan. Reheat syrup and repeat process 3 times. Pack into hot sterilized jars, leaving ½ inch headspace; seal with 2-piece lids. Process in boiling water bath for 10 minutes. Yield: 6 quarts.

Mary Seffert, Texas

Sweet and Sour Pineapple Pickles

2 medium fresh pineapples
2 cups packed light brown sugar
1 cup cider vinegar

2 cups water
1 (3-inch) cinnamon stick
2 tablespoons whole cloves

Peel pineapple. Cut into spears, discarding core. Combine brown sugar, cider vinegar and water in large saucepan. Tie cinnamon stick and cloves in cheesecloth. Add to vinegar mixture. Bring to a boil. Cook for 5 minutes. Add pineapple. Simmer, covered, for 5 minutes. Remove spice bag. Pack pineapple into hot sterilized jars, leaving ½ inch headspace; seal with 2-piece lids. Process in boiling water bath for 15 minutes. Yield: 3 pints.

Lena Marchetti, Pennsylvania

Zucchini Pickles

24 medium zucchini	3 cups vinegar
1/4 cup pickling salt	1/3 cup mustard seed
3 cups sugar	4 teaspoons celery seed

Cut zucchini into quarters. Cut quarters into 3-inch sticks. Place in large nonmetallic bowl. Sprinkle with pickling salt. Add enough cold water to cover. Let stand for 3 hours. Drain; rinse well. Combine sugar, vinegar, mustard seed and celery seed in large saucepan. Bring to a boil over medium heat. Add zucchini; reduce heat. Cook over low heat for 5 minutes; do not bring to a boil. Pack zucchini into hot sterilized 1-pint jars; leave 1/2 inch headspace. Pour in hot liquid, leaving 1/2 inch headspace. Seal with 2-piece lids. Process in boiling water bath for 10 minutes. Yield: 9 pints.

Anne Rice, Kansas

Pepper and Cucumber Relish

2 green bell peppers, ground	1 cup cider vinegar
2 red bell peppers, ground	1/2 cup water
8 cups ground cucumbers	3 cups sugar
4 cups ground onions	2 tablespoons white mustard
1/4 cup salt	seed
1 cup cider vinegar	1 teaspoon whole allspice
2 cups water	1 1/2 teaspoons peppercorn.

Combine ground vegetables and salt in bowl; mix well. Let stand at room temperature overnight. Drain well. Combine 1 cup cider vinegar and 2 cups water in saucepan. Add vegetables. Bring to a boil. Cook for 15 minutes. Drain. Add 1 cup cider vinegar, 1/2 cup water, sugar and spices. Bring to a boil. Cook for 15 minutes. Spoon into hot sterilized jars, leaving 1/2 inch headspace; seal with 2-piece lids. Process in boiling water bath for 10 minutes. Cool. Yield: 8 pints.

Sally Milligan, Tennessee

Apple and Beet Relish

6 cups chopped cooked beets
6 cups chopped peeled apples
2 large onions, cut into quarters
1¹/2 cups sugar

1¹/2 cups vinegar
2 (2-inch) cinnamon sticks
¹/2 cup water

Shred beets, apples and onions in food processor container. Combine with sugar, vinegar, cinnamon sticks and water in large saucepan. Simmer, covered, for 20 to 25 minutes, stirring frequently. Remove cinnamon sticks. Ladle into hot sterilized ¹/2-pint jars, leaving ¹/2 inch headspace; seal with 2-piece lids. Process in boiling water bath for 15 minutes. Yield: 5¹/2 pints.

Kathy Pelham, Missouri

Easy Marinated Olives

2 (5-ounce) jars stuffed Spanish
   olives, drained
2 (6-ounce) cans pitted black
   olives, drained
6 fresh basil leaves or 1
   tablespoon dried basil

2 large cloves of garlic
6 tablespoons tarragon vinegar
6 tablespoons wine vinegar
¹/2 teaspoon pepper
³/4 cup olive oil

Place olives in bowl. Add basil and garlic. Combine vinegars, pepper and oil in bowl; mix well. Pour over olives. Marinate, covered, in the refrigerator for 3 days or longer. Pack into decorative gift jars. Drain olives and discard garlic before serving. Yield: 4 cups.

Bonnie Lindt, Nebraska

Hot Fudge Sauce

²/3 cup semisweet chocolate
   chips
2 tablespoons butter or
   margarine

¹/8 teaspoon salt
1 (14-ounce) can sweetened
   condensed milk
1 teaspoon vanilla extract

Melt chocolate and butter in heavy saucepan over low heat, stirring constantly. Stir in salt and sweetened condensed milk. Cook for 5 minutes or until slightly thickened, stirring constantly. Blend in vanilla. Serve warm or cold over ice cream. Yield: 1¹/2 cups.

Coralee Rowles, Virginia

Jezebel Sauce

1 (10-ounce) jar apricot
  preserves
1 (6-ounce) jar cream-style
  horseradish

1 (10-ounce) jar apple jelly
1/2 (1 1/2-ounce) can dry mustard
1 teaspoon pepper

Combine apricot preserves, horseradish, apple jelly, dry mustard and pepper in saucepan. Bring to a boil, stirring constantly. Cool. Pour mixture into decorative jars; seal. Store jars in refrigerator. Serve over cream cheese as spread or as relish for ham or pork. Yield: 3 cups.

Donna Roberts, Georgia

Cranberry Tea Mix

1 (16-ounce) package fresh
  cranberries
4 cups water
12 whole cloves
3 1/2 cups sugar

1 cup red hot cinnamon candies
4 cups water
Juice of 2 oranges
Juice of 1/2 lemon

Combine cranberries and 4 cups water in saucepan. Cook until cranberries are tender. Strain through cheesecloth into pitcher, reserving cranberries for another use. Tie cloves in cheesecloth. Combine with sugar, candies and 4 cups water in saucepan. Boil for 5 minutes. Remove cloves. Stir in cranberry juice, orange juice and lemon juice. Store in refrigerator for up to 4 weeks. Combine equal parts cranberry syrup and water in saucepan. Heat to serving temperature. Yield: 16 to 24 servings.

Ginny Porterhouse, Florida

Cocoa Mix

8 cups nonfat dry milk powder
1 (10-ounce) jar instant
  nondairy creamer

1 (16-ounce) package instant
  cocoa mix
1 1/2 cups confectioners' sugar

Combine dry milk powder, creamer, cocoa mix and confectioners' sugar in bowl; mix well. Store in airtight container. Give with instructions to mix 1/3 to 1/2 cup cocoa mix with 1 cup boiling water for each serving. Garnish with marshmallows and peppermint stick stirrers if desired. Yield: 24 to 36 servings.

Lorna Hamlisch, Wisconsin

French Market Soup Mix

1 pound dried black-eyed peas
1 pound split peas
1 pound dried lentils
1 pound dried black beans
1 pound dried baby lima beans

1 pound dried kidney beans
1 pound dried Great Northern
  beans
1 pound dried navy beans
2 cups pearl barley

Layer 1/4 cup each ingredient in glass 1-pint jars; seal. Include soup recipe with each gift, or assemble baskets with soup mix, soup ingredients and copy of recipe. Yield: 8 pints.

French Market Bean Soup

1 jar French Market Soup Mix
6 cups water
8 cups water
1 pound cooked ham, chopped
1 onion, chopped
2 cloves of garlic, minced

1 bay leaf
1/2 teaspoon oregano
8 ounces kielbasa, sliced
1 (16-ounce) can tomatoes
1 (10-ounce) can Ro-Tel
  tomatoes and green chilies

Soak Soup Mix in 6 cups water in saucepan overnight; drain. Add 8 cups water, ham, onion, garlic, bay leaf and oregano. Simmer, covered, for 1 1/2 hours or until beans are tender. Remove bay leaf. Add sausage and undrained tomatoes. Simmer for 30 minutes. Ladle into soup bowls. Yield: 10 servings.

Polly Spellman, South Carolina

Fruited Curried Rice Mix

4 cups long grain rice
2 cups chopped dried fruit
2 cups slivered almonds
1 cup golden raisins
1/4 cup dried minced onion

8 teaspoons curry powder
8 teaspoons instant beef
  bouillon
2 teaspoons salt

Combine 1 cup rice, 1/2 cup fruit, 1/2 cup almonds, 1/4 cup raisins, 1 tablespoon onion, 2 teaspoons each curry powder and bouillon and 1/2 teaspoon salt in four 1-pint airtight containers. Include the following directions with each gift: Combine 1 jar rice mix with 2 1/2 cups water and 2 tablespoons butter in covered saucepan. Bring to a boil; reduce heat. Simmer for 20 minutes. Yield: 4 pints.

Rose Sahota, Michigan

Wild Rice Pilaf Mix

3 cups wild rice
2 cups dried lentils
1   (15-ounce) package raisins
1¹/2 cups chopped dried
    mushrooms
1 cup barley
¹/2 cup hulled sunflower seed
10 tablespoons instant beef
    bouillon

10 tablespoons dried parsley
    flakes
1¹/4 cups instant minced onion
2¹/2 teaspoons basil
2¹/2 teaspoons garlic powder
5 teaspoons salt
2¹/2 teaspoons pepper
1¹/2 teaspoons (about)
    cinnamon

Preheat oven to 350 degrees. Rinse and drain wild rice. Spread in single layer on baking sheet. Bake for 10 to 15 minutes or until dry. Cool. Combine wild rice, lentils, raisins, mushrooms, barley and sunflower seed in bowl; mix well. Divide into 1 cup portions; place in 10 small jars. Add 1 tablespoon bouillon, 1 tablespoon parsley flakes, 2 tablespoons minced onion, ¹/4 teaspoon basil, ¹/4 teaspoon garlic powder, ¹/2 teaspoon salt, ¹/2 teaspoon pepper and pinch of cinnamon to each jar; seal. Give with recipe for Wild Rice Pilaf. Yield: 10 cups.

Wild Rice Pilaf

3 cups water
1 cup Wild Rice Pilaf Mix

4 to 6 carrots, peeled, chopped

Bring water to a boil in saucepan. Add Pilaf Mix and carrots. Bring to a boil over high heat; cover and reduce heat to low. Simmer for 50 minutes or until wild rice is tender. Adjust seasonings before serving.
Yield: 6 servings.

Jessie Morris, Indiana

Creole Seasoning Mix

1   (26-ounce) container salt
1   (1¹/2-ounce) can black pepper
1   (2-ounce) jar red pepper

1   (10-ounce) jar garlic powder
1   (1-ounce) package chili
    powder

Combine salt, black pepper, red pepper, garlic powder and chili powder in plastic bag; seal. Shake until well mixed. Package in airtight containers or glass shakers for gifts. Yield: 40 ounces.

Abby Waldrup, California

Cheesy Seasoning Mix

2 cups Parmesan cheese
1/2 cup sesame seed
1/2 teaspoon garlic salt
1 tablespoon instant minced
   onion
1/2 teaspoon dillseed

2 tablespoons parsley flakes
2 tablespoons poppy seed
3 tablespoons celery seed
2 teaspoons paprika
1/2 teaspoon pepper

Combine cheese, sesame seed, garlic salt, instant onion, dillseed, parsley flakes, poppy seed, celery seed, paprika and pepper in plastic bag; seal. Shake to mix well. Package in airtight containers to give as gifts. Yield: 3 cups.

Julie Schull, Illinois

Dilled Seasoning Salt

1 (26-ounce) container salt
1 tablespoon onion salt
1 tablespoon garlic salt
2 tablespoons celery salt
2 tablespoons paprika

1/4 cup black pepper
1/4 cup white pepper
1 tablespoon dillweed
1/4 cup sugar

Combine salt, onion salt, garlic salt, celery salt, paprika, black pepper, white pepper, dillweed and sugar in bowl; mix well. Let stand, covered, in dark place for 24 hours. Package in salt shakers or spice jars for gifts. Yield: 3 cups.

Cynthia Threilkeld, Oklahoma

Coconut Granola Snack

2 2/3 cups flaked coconut
1 cup quick-cooking oats
1/4 cup packed light brown
   sugar
1/4 cup chopped dried apricots

1/4 cup chopped prunes
2 tablespoons sesame seed
1/4 cup oil
1/4 cup honey
1/4 cup seedless raisins

Preheat oven to 325 degrees. Combine coconut, oats, brown sugar, apricots, prunes and sesame seed in large bowl; mix well. Mix oil and honey in saucepan. Bring to a boil over medium heat. Pour over fruit mixture; mix well. Spread evenly in 10x15-inch baking pan. Bake for 30 minutes, stirring frequently; do not brown. Stir in raisins. Let stand until cool, stirring occasionally to break granola apart. Store in airtight container. Yield: 7 cups.

Inez Lopez, Texas

Microwave Granola

1/2 cup sunflower oil
1/2 cup honey
1 cup packed light brown sugar
2 teaspoons cinnamon
2 teaspoons vanilla extract
6 cups oats
1 cup coconut
1/2 cup wheat germ
1/2 cup sunflower seed

1/2 cup dry milk powder
1 cup blanched chopped
   almonds
2/3 cup raisins
2/3 cup dried apples, chopped
2/3 cup dried apricots, chopped
2/3 cup dates, chopped
2/3 cup dried pineapple,
   chopped

Combine oil, honey, brown sugar, cinnamon and vanilla in glass dish. Microwave on High for 4 to 5 minutes or until brown sugar is melted, stirring once. Add oats, coconut, wheat germ, sunflower seed, milk powder and almonds; mix well. Divide into 2 portions. Microwave each portion for 12 minutes or until mixture begins to appear dry, stirring several times. Stir in raisins, apples, apricots, dates and pineapple. Spread on waxed paper to cool. Package in airtight container. Yield: 5 cups.

Denise Maddox, Alabama

Snacker Crackers

3/4 cup safflower oil
1 (11/2-ounce) package dry blue
   cheese salad dressing mix
1 teaspoon parsley flakes

1 teaspoon dillweed
1/2 teaspoon garlic powder
1 (16-ounce) package oyster
   crackers

Combine oil, salad dressing mix, parsley, dillweed and garlic powder in small bowl; mix well. Place oyster crackers in larger bowl. Pour oil mixture over crackers; mix well. Store, tightly covered, for 3 days; stir mixture twice a day. Package in airtight containers for gifts. Yield: 5 cups.

Hazel McNutt, Colorado

Nibbles and Bits

1 cup confectioners' sugar	1 (12-ounce) package Crispix
2 cups milk chocolate chips	cereal
1 cup creamy peanut butter	1 cup confectioners' sugar

Place 1 cup confectioners' sugar in paper bag. Melt chocolate chips with peanut butter in large skillet over low heat, stirring constantly. Add cereal; stir gently until cereal is coated. Place cereal and remaining confectioners' sugar in paper bag; shake until well coated. Spread in single layer on waxed paper or on foil-lined tray. Let stand until cool. Package in airtight containers for gifts. Yield: 10 cups.

Velma Rogers, Tennessee

Praline Nibbles

3/4 cup butter or margarine	2 cups rice Chex
3/4 cup packed light brown	2 cups corn Chex
sugar	2 cups wheat Chex
1 cup pecans, broken	

Preheat oven to 325 degrees. Combine butter and brown sugar in saucepan. Bring to a boil. Cook for 2 minutes; remove from heat. Stir in pecans and cereal. Place in 9x13-inch baking pan. Bake for 8 minutes. Stir to mix well. Bake for 8 minutes longer. Stir to mix well. Cool on paper towels. Yield: 7 cups.

Patricia Damon, Louisiana

Mexican Party Mix

1 (20-ounce) package Crispix	1/2 cup Parmesan cheese
cereal	5 tablespoons Worcestershire
1 (8-ounce) package small	sauce
pretzels	Garlic salt to taste
1 (8-ounce) package corn spirals	1 tablespoon chili powder
2 cups mixed nuts	1 cup melted butter or
2 envelopes dry taco seasoning	margarine
mix	

Preheat oven to 225 degrees. Combine cereal, pretzels, corn spirals and nuts in baking pan; mix well. Sprinkle with dry taco seasoning mix,

Parmesan cheese, Worcestershire sauce, garlic salt and chili powder. Drizzle with butter. Toss to mix well. Bake for 45 minutes, stirring every 15 minutes. Cool. Store in airtight container. Yield: 24 servings.

Kelly Wellman, Washington

Fancy Party Mix

1 (12-ounce) package rice Chex
1 (12-ounce) package corn Chex
1 (12-ounce) package wheat Chex
1 (14-ounce) package honey-nut oat cereal
1 (12-ounce) package miniature pretzels
1 (14-ounce) package cheese crackers
1 (11-ounce) package corn chips
2 cups pecan halves

1 (16-pounce) jar Spanish peanuts
1 (16-ounce) jar mixed nuts
2 cups melted butter or margarine
1 teaspoon chili powder
1 tablespoon Tabasco sauce
1 tablespoon Worcestershire sauce
1 teaspoon garlic powder
Seasoning salt to taste

Preheat oven to 250 degrees. Combine cereals, pretzels, crackers, corn chips and nuts in large bowl; mix lightly. Spread in 2 large roasting pans. Mix butter and seasonings in bowl. Pour over cereal mixture; mix lightly. Bake for 1 hour, stirring frequently. Cool. Store in airtight containers. Yield: 50 cups.

Annette Gray, Mississippi

Oriental Almonds

2 cups whole almonds
1 tablespoon honey

1 tablespoon soy sauce
1 teaspoon soybean oil

Preheat oven to 350 degrees. Spread almonds in single layer on ungreased baking sheet. Toast for 15 minutes; do not stir. Cool. Reduce oven temperature to 250 degrees. Mix honey and soy sauce in medium saucepan. Bring to a boil over low heat. Add almonds. Cook for 2 to 3 minutes, stirring constantly; remove from heat. Sprinkle with oil; toss to mix. Spread in single layer on baking sheet; separate almonds. Bake for 5 minutes; stir carefully. Bake for 5 minutes longer or to desired brown color; watch carefully during last 5 minutes of baking time to prevent overbrowning. Cool. Pack in decorative airtight containers. Yield: 2 cups.

Lindsey Haveman, Michigan

Frosted Pecans

1 egg white
1 teaspoon cold water
1 pound large pecan halves

1 cup sugar
1 teaspoon cinnamon
1 teaspoon salt

Preheat oven to 225 degrees. Beat egg white with water in mixer bowl until frothy. Stir in pecans. Mix remaining ingredients in small bowl. Add to pecans; mix well. Spread on baking sheet. Bake for 1 hour, stirring occasionally. Cool. Place in decorative airtight containers.
Yield: 1 pound.

Frances Brillian, New York

Microwave Worcestershire Pecans

1 tablespoon melted butter or
   margarine
2 tablespoons Worcestershire
   sauce

Dash of Tabasco sauce
1¹/₂ cups pecan halves
Salt and pepper to taste

Mix butter, Worcestershire sauce and Tabasco sauce in glass bowl. Stir in pecans, coating well. Microwave on High for 5 to 6 minutes, stirring twice. Sprinkle with salt and pepper. Cool. Store in decorative airtight container. Yield: 1¹/₂ cups.

Martha Donaldson, Georgia

Roasted Rosemary Walnuts

2 quarts water
1 pound broken walnuts
¹/₄ cup melted butter or
   margarine

¹/₂ teaspoon salt
¹/₈ teaspoon pepper
1 tablespoon dried rosemary
   leaves, crushed

Preheat oven to 275 degrees. Bring water to a boil in large saucepan over high heat. Add walnuts. Return to a boil. Boil for 1 minute. Pour into colander; rinse under hot running water. Drain well. Spread in single layer in 10x15-inch baking pan. Bake for 30 minutes or until dry. Stir frequently. Drizzle with butter; sprinkle with salt, pepper and rosemary. Bake for 20 minutes or until brown and crisp, stirring frequently. Cool. Pack in airtight containers for gifts. Yield: 4 cups.

Nora Thweatt, Nebraska

Spicy Toasted Nuts

2 tablespoons butter
2 tablespoons sugar
1 teaspoon garlic salt

1/2 teaspoon curry powder
1/2 teaspoon cinnamon
4 cups mixed nuts

Preheat oven to 350 degrees. Melt butter in small saucepan. Stir in sugar, garlic salt, curry powder and cinnamon. Place nuts in 9x9-inch baking pan. Pour butter mixture over nuts; mix to coat well. Bake, uncovered, for 20 minutes or until butter sizzles. Stir to coat well. Let stand until cool, stirring frequently. Store in airtight container. Yield: 4 cups.

Sarah Grigsby, North Carolina

Popcorn Balls

12 cups popped popcorn
2 cups chopped gumdrops
1 cup chopped nuts
1 cup light corn syrup
1/2 cup honey

1 1/2 teaspoons vinegar
3/4 teaspoon salt
1 tablespoon butter or
  margarine
1 1/2 teaspoons vanilla extract

Combine popcorn, gumdrops and nuts in bowl. Mix corn syrup, honey, vinegar and salt in saucepan. Bring to a boil over medium heat. Cook to 260 to 265 degrees on candy thermometer, hard-ball stage. Stir in butter and vanilla. Pour over popcorn mixture; mix well. Shape into 2-inch balls. Place on waxed paper-lined surface. Let stand until firm. Wrap individually in plastic wrap. Yield: 2 1/2 dozen.

Eunice Walls, West Virginia

Poppycock

1 cup melted butter
2 cups sugar
1/2 cup light corn syrup
1 teaspoon salt
1 teaspoon vanilla extract

1/2 teaspoon soda
5 quarts popped popcorn
1 cup almonds
1 cup pecan halves

Bring butter, sugar, corn syrup and salt to a boil in saucepan, stirring constantly. Cook for 5 minutes; do not stir. Remove from heat. Stir in vanilla and soda. Pour over popcorn and nuts in large bowl; mix well. Spread in two 9x13-inch baking pans. Bake for 1 to 1 1/2 hours, stirring every 20 minutes. Store in airtight containers. Yield: 12 cups.

Alice Joyner, Louisiana

Poppy Seed Sticks

1/4 cup butter, softened
1 cup Parmesan cheese
3/4 cup sour cream
1/2 teaspoon Italian seasoning
1 cup all-purpose flour

1 egg yolk
1 egg white
1 tablespoon water
2 tablespoons poppy seed

Preheat oven to 350 degrees. Combine butter and Parmesan cheese in bowl; mix well. Add 1/2 cup sour cream; mix well. Add enough remaining sour cream to make texture light and fluffy. Add Italian seasoning, flour and egg yolk; mix well. Roll dough 1/2 at a time on lightly floured surface. Cut into 1/2x6-inch strips. Mix egg white and water. Brush over breadsticks. Sprinkle with poppy seed. Twist each strip several times. Place on greased baking sheet. Bake for 30 minutes or until light brown. Cool on wire rack. Store in loosely covered container. May substitute caraway seed or coarse salt for poppy seed. Yield: 1 1/2 dozen.

Lee Alcorn, Maryland

Caramel Popcorn

2 quarts popped popcorn
1/2 cup butter or margarine
3/4 cup packed light brown
   sugar

1/4 cup light corn syrup
2 teaspoons vanilla extract
1/4 teaspoon soda
1 cup chopped nuts

Preheat oven to 250 degrees. Place popcorn in large heatproof bowl in oven. Melt butter in large heavy saucepan. Add sugar and corn syrup. Bring to a boil, stirring constantly. Boil over medium heat for 5 minutes; do not stir. Remove from heat. Stir in vanilla and soda quickly. Pour over popcorn, stirring until coated. Mix in nuts. Pour into greased 10x15-inch baking pan. Bake for 1 hour, stirring every 15 minutes. Cool. Break into pieces. Store in airtight container. Yield: 8 cups.

Edith Felner, Arkansas

Gifts from Helping Hands

♥ *Gifts of Caring* ♥

*A*ll of us have experienced a time or two in our lives when we've heaved a sigh and wished dinner would miraculously appear on the doorstep that night. The trauma that day may have been nothing more than a busy day at the local mall; or it may have been the first day home from the hospital with twins.

Whatever the circumstances, no gift can be more appreciated than a ready-to-enjoy meal during busy or stressful times.

A caring gift from our kitchens lends support in more ways than one. Not only is homemade food a delicious convenience when it's most needed, it can also be nourishing psychologically and emotionally – as worldwide sentiment about the value of chicken soup attests.

Nearly all of us think about sending good things to eat to sick friends or shut-ins, new moms, recent arrivals in the neighborhood or those in the midst of serious crisis. But "helping hands" gifts are just as meaningful during those daily little crises: to the friend who's entertaining a horde of out-of-town company; or the neighbors who just found out they need a new water heater.

If you're like most of us, you've probably developed a few tried and true dishes you've sent as gifts for years. Hold on to them: they're the stuff classics are made of. But there's no need to limit yourself to the same old standbys, either. In the following pages, you'll find delectable recipes for stand-out main dishes, as well as unusual salads and side dishes that will really make the meal. And high on the list of most-loved gifts are our dessert creations, guaranteed to brighten up even the dreariest day–not just for the recipient of the gift, but for yourself as well.

♥ *Main Dish Helpers* ♥

Steak Roulades

12 (¹/₄x3x5-inch) pieces round
    steak
Salt and pepper to taste
Mushroom Stuffing
1 cup (about) all-purpose flour

¹/₄ cup butter or margarine
²/₃ cup chopped celery
¹/₂ cup sliced mushrooms
2 cups beef broth
1 cup sour cream

Preheat oven to 350 degrees. Pound round steak very thin with meat mallet. Sprinkle with salt and pepper. Place 2 tablespoons Mushroom Stuffing on each piece. Roll as for jelly roll; tie with butcher's string. Coat with flour. Brown several at a time on all sides in butter in Dutch oven for 5 to 7 minutes. Drain on paper towel. Add celery and mushrooms to Dutch oven. Stir-fry for 2 minutes. Add steak rolls and broth; cover tightly. Bake for 1¹/₂ hours or until tender. Place roulades on heated serving plate; remover butcher's string. Stir sour cream into pan juices. Heat to serving temperature; do not boil. Spoon over steak rolls. Serve with remaining gravy. Yield: 12 servings.

Mushroom Stuffing

1 cup chopped onion
2 tablespoons butter or
    margarine
¹/₂ cup chopped mushrooms
2 cups soft bread crumbs

12 cup water
1 egg
¹/₂ teaspoon salt
¹/₈ teaspoon pepper
2 tablespoons minced parsley

Sauté onion in butter in skillet until golden brown. Add mushrooms. Sauté for 1 minute. Remove from heat. Add bread crumbs, water, egg and seasonings; mix well.

Margaret Sevier, Florida

Easy Beef Bake

2 pounds boneless round steak
2 tablespoons vegetable oil
1½ cups chopped onion
1 bay leaf
1 can cream of chicken soup
1 can onion soup
½ cup all-purpose flour

1 tablespoon Worcestershire
  sauce
1 (4-ounce) can sliced
  mushrooms, drained
1 (10-ounce) package frozen
  peas, thawed
6 green bell pepper rings

Preheat oven to 350 degrees. Cut steak into 1-inch cubes. Brown steak in oil in 3-quart Dutch oven. Sprinkle with onion. Add bay leaf. Combine soups, flour, Worcestershire sauce and mushrooms in bowl; mix well. Pour over steak. Bake, covered, for 2 hours or until tender. Remove bay leaf. Add peas. Top with green pepper rings. Bake, covered, for 20 minutes longer. Yield: 6 servings.

Melissa Regelean, Texas

Burgundy Beef

3 pounds lean beef
1½ punds mushrooms
1 pound carrots
1 pound small white onions
1 bunch celery
6 slices bacon
2 tablespoons corn oil
1 cup dry red wine

2 teaspoons sugar
1 teaspoon salt
¼ teaspoon pepper
1 teaspoon instant beef bouillon
1¼ cups water
2 tablespoons all-purpose flour
¼ cup water
1 tablespoon minced parsley

Cut beef into 1½-inch cubes. Cut mushrooms into halves. Peel and chop carrots. Peel onions. Chop celery and bacon. Brown beef ½ at a time in oil in 5-quart saucepan over medium-high heat. Remove beef with slotted spoon. Sauté mushrooms in pan drippings, adding a small amount of additional oil if necessary. Remove with slotted spoon. Add carrots, onions, celery and bacon. Sauté until vegetables are browned. Add wine, sugar, salt, pepper, bouillon, 1¼ cups water and beef. Bring to a boil; reduce heat. Simmer, covered, over low heat for 1½ hours or until beef is tender, stirring occasionally. Add mushrooms. Cook for 15 minutes. Skim fat. Blend flour and ¼ cup water in small bowl. Stir into beef mixture. Cook over medium heat until thickened, stirring constantly. Garnish with parsley. Yield: 12 servings.

Ruth Claxton, Kentucky

Italian Beef Stew

3 pounds cubed lean beef
3 tablespoons olive oil
1 cup chopped onion
4 ounces cooked ham, slivered
1 clove of garlic, minced
1 (28-ounce) can tomatoes
2 tablespoons wine vinegar

2 teaspoons basil
2 teaspoons salt
1/4 teaspoon pepper
1 (14-ounce) can artichoke
   hearts in brine, drained
1 (10-ounce) package frozen
   peas, thawed

Preheat oven to 325 degrees. Brown beef in olive oil in Dutch oven; remove with slotted spoon. Sauté onion, ham and garlic in pan drippings over medium heat for 2 minutes. Stir in tomatoes, vinegar and seasonings. Add browned beef. Bake, covered, for 2 1/2 hours or until beef is tender; skim. Add artichoke hearts and peas. Bake, covered, for 15 minutes longer. Yield: 8 servings.

Marian Miles, North Carolina

Chili Fiesta

6 dried chili peppers
3 1/2 cups beef broth
1 large onion, chopped
4 large cloves of garlic, minced
1/2 teaspoon salt
2 tablespoons corn oil
3 pounds lean beef cubes
1 to 3 tablespoons chili powder
2 teaspoons ground cumin

1 to 2 tablespoons cornmeal
3 cups hot cooked rice
1 cup chopped red onion
1 large tomato, chopped
1 medium avocado, peeled,
   chopped
2 limes, cut into wedges
2 cups shredded Cheddar
   cheese

Seed and coarsely chop chilies. Wash hands well after handling chilies; do not touch face or eyes. Combine chilies with boiling beef broth in bowl. Let stand for 30 minutes. Sauté onion, garlic and salt in oil in heavy saucepan until light brown. Add beef. Sauté just until beef loses pink color. Strain chilies, reserving both broth and chilies. Stir 2 1/2 cups chili broth, chili powder and cumin into beef mixture. Bring to a boil; reduce heat to medium-low. Simmer, uncovered, for 1 hour, stirring occasionally. Combine softened chilies, remaining chili broth and a small amount of water if necessary in blender container. Process until smooth. Add to beef mixture. Simmer for 30 minutes, stirring occasionally. Add cornmeal gradually. Cook until thickened, stirring constantly. Add salt to taste. Top servings with rice, red onion, tomato, avocado, lime wedges and cheese. Yield: 12 servings.

Barb Dell, Connecticut

Baked Stroganoff

3 pounds round steak
1 cup dry red wine
1 envelope dry onion soup mix
2 (8-ounce) cans sliced
  mushrooms
1 can cream of chicken soup
1 can cream of celery soup

1 can cream of mushroom soup
1 teaspoon salt
1/2 teaspoon pepper
2 cups sour cream
1 (16-ounce) package wide
  noodles, cooked

Preheat oven to 300 degrees. Cut round steak into cubes. Combine steak with wine, dry soup mix, mushrooms, canned soups, salt and pepper in roasting pan; mix well. Bake for 3 to 4 hours or until steak is very tender. Stir in sour cream just before serving. Serve over noodles.
Yield: 10 servings.

Nancy Fouvier, Louisiana

Ground Beef and Green Chili Bake

1 pound ground beef
1/2 cup chopped onion
2 (4-ounce) cans chopped green
  chilies
1 cup shredded Monterey Jack
  cheese

4 eggs
1 1/2 cups milk
1/4 cup all-purpose flour
1/2 cup shredded Monterey Jack
  cheese

Preheat oven to 350 degrees. Brown ground beef with onion in skillet, stirring until ground beef is crumbly; drain. Layer ground beef, green chilies and 1 cup cheese in greased 6x10-inch baking dish. Beat eggs with milk and flour in bowl. Pour over layers. Top with 1/2 cup cheese. Bake for 45 minutes or until set. Let stand for 5 minutes. Cut into squares.
Yield: 6 servings.

Donna Brooks, Arizona

♥ *For a quick Beef Stroganoff, brown 1 pound of sirloin steak strips with 1 chopped onion, and stir in 1 cup of water and 1 package of mushroom gravy mix. Simmer for 30 minutes. Serve over rice or noodles with sour cream.*

Ground Beef and Noodles Florentine

2 pounds ground beef
3/4 cup chopped onion
1 (8-ounce) can tomato sauce
1/4 teaspoon nutmeg
1/2 teaspoon salt
1/8 teaspoon pepper
1/4 cup butter or margarine
1/2 cup all-purpose flour
1/2 teaspoon salt
3 cups milk

8 ounces wide noodles
2 (10-ounce) packages frozen
  chopped spinach, thawed,
  drained
1/2 cup shredded Cheddar
  cheese
2 tablespoons Parmesan cheese
1/4 cup shredded Cheddar
  cheese

Preheat oven to 350 degrees. Brown ground beef and onion in large skillet, stirring until ground beef is crumbly; drain. Stir in tomato sauce, nutmeg, 1/2 teaspoon salt and pepper. Simmer for 10 minutes. Melt butter in saucepan. Blend in flour and 1/2 teaspoon salt. Stir in milk gradually. Cook until thickened, stirring constantly. Cook noodles according to package directions; drain. Stir into white sauce. Spread half the noodle mixture into 9x13-inch baking dish. Layer 2/3 of the ground beef mixture, the spinach, 1/2 cup Cheddar cheese and remaining noodle mixture in dish. Top with remaining ground beef mixture. Bake, covered, for 25 minutes. Sprinkle with Parmesan cheese and 1/4 cup Cheddar cheese. Bake for 5 minutes longer. Let stand for 10 minutes before serving. Yield: 8 servings.

Opal Griffith, Texas

Honey-Glazed Meatballs

1/4 cup finely chopped onion
1 pound lean ground beef
3/4 cup fresh bread crumbs
1 egg
1 teaspoon salt
1/4 teaspoon pepper

1 tablespoon all-purpose flour
1 cup orange juice
1 1/2 teaspoons lemon juice
1/4 cup Drambuie
1/4 cup honey
1 orange, sliced

Preheat oven to 350 degrees. Combine onion, ground beef, bread crumbs, egg, salt and pepper in bowl; mix well. Shape into 1-inch meatballs. Place in 10x15-inch baking pan. Blend flour and a small amount of orange juice in saucepan. Stir in remaining orange juice, lemon juice, Drambuie and honey gradually. Bring to a boil, stirring constantly. Brush meatballs with glaze. Bake for 25 minutes or until brown, brushing with remaining glaze 2 times. Garnish with orange slices. Yield: 2 dozen.

Gail Siegfried, Indiana

Taco Pie

2 cups mashed potatoes
1/4 cup melted butter or
  margarine
1/2 cup milk
1 (1¼-ounce) package taco
  seasoning mix
1 pound ground beef

1/2 cup chopped onion
1 (16-ounce) can refried beans
1/2 cup taco sauce
1/4 cup water
1 cup shredded Cheddar cheese
1 cup shredded lettuce
1 medium tomato, chopped

Preheat oven to 350 degrees. Combine potatoes, butter, milk and 2 tablespoons taco seasoning mix in bowl; mix well. Press over bottom and side of 10-inch pie plate to form shell. Brown ground beef and onion in skillet, stirring until crumbly; drain well. Add remaining taco seasoning mix, beans, taco sauce and water; mix well. Spoon into potato shell. Bake for 30 minutes. Top with cheese, lettuce and tomato. Yield: 6 servings.

Deborah Fenner, Wisconsin

Glazed Beef Roll

3/4 cup chopped onion
1 tablespoon butter or
  margarine
1½ cups shredded carrots
1/4 teaspoon salt
1½ pounds lean ground beef
1½ cups soft bread crumbs
1 egg, beaten
2 tablespoons milk

3/4 teaspoon salt
3/4 teaspoon thyme
1/8 teaspoon garlic powder
Pepper to taste
1 (16-ounce) jar spiced crab
  apples
1/3 cup pineapple preserves
1 teaspoon mustard

Preheat oven to 350 degrees. Sauté onion in butter in skillet until tender. Cook carrots in a small amount of water in saucepan for 5 minutes; drain. Mix carrots with half the sautéed onion and 1/4 teaspoon salt; set aside. Combine ground beef, bread crumbs, remaining sautéed onion, egg, milk, 3/4 teaspoon salt, thyme, garlic powder and pepper in bowl; mix well. Shape into 8x10-inch rectangle on waxed paper. Spread carrot mixture to within 1 inch of edge; roll as for jelly roll, sealing edge. Place seam side down in 9x13-inch baking dish. Bake for 1 hour; drain drippings. Drain crab apples, reserving 1 cup liquid. Mix reserved liquid, preserves and mustard in saucepan. Simmer for 15 minutes. Spoon over meat roll. Bake for 15 minutes longer. Remove to serving platter. Place crab apples around roll. Let stand for 10 minutes before slicing. Yield: 8 servings.

Gladys Simonson, Washington

Baked Spanish Stew

3/4 cup pearl barley
1 1/2 cups water
1 pound lean ground beef
1/2 cup chopped onion
1/2 cup chopped celery
1/2 cup chopped green bell
   pepper
2 tablespoons olive oil
1 (28-ounce) can tomatoes
1/2 cup chili sauce

1 teaspoon Worcestershire sauce
1 teaspoon sugar
1/2 teaspoon marjoram
Salt and pepper to taste
1/2 cup shredded Cheddar
   cheese
1/2 cup sliced black olives
1 (7-ounce) package tortilla
   chips

Simmer barley in water in covered saucepan for 30 minutes. Preheat oven to 350 degrees. Sauté ground beef, onion, celery and green pepper in oil in skillet. Add barley, tomatoes, chili sauce, Worcestershire sauce, sugar and seasonings; mix well. Simmer for 10 minutes. Pour into 3-quart baking dish. Sprinkle cheese and olives over top. Arrange tortilla chips around edge. Bake for 20 minutes or until cheese is bubbly. Yield: 6 to 8 servings.

Kay Meyer, Maryland

Dijon Ham

1 (3-pound) canned ham
1/4 cup Dijon-style mustard
Whole cloves
1/3 cup orange marmalade

1/4 cup maple syrup
2 tablespoons cider vinegar
1 cup red wine
1/3 cup cola

Preheat oven to 350 degrees. Place ham in shallow baking dish. Spread with mustard. Stud with cloves. Spoon marmalade over ham. Drizzle with maple syrup and mixture of cider vinegar, wine and cola. Bake for 1 hour, basting every 15 minutes. Let stand for 15 minutes before slicing. Yield: 8 servings.

Virginia Petty, South Carolina

♥ *For an especially festive dish, slice canned ham; spoon prepared stuffing mix between every 2 slices. Tie together and bake as above.*

Ham Loaves

1 pound ground ham	1 tablespoon Worcestershire
1 pound lean ground pork	sauce
1 pound lean ground beef	1/2 teaspoon Tabasco sauce
2 eggs	1 can tomato soup
1 cup quick-cooking oats	2 tablespoons light brown sugar
1 cup milk	1/2 teaspoon ground cloves
1 teaspoon dry mustard	1/2 teaspoon chili powder

Combine ham, pork, beef, eggs, oats, milk, mustard, Worcestershire sauce, Tabasco sauce and 1/2 cup tomato soup in bowl; mix well. Mixture will be moist. Press into two 5x9-inch loaf pans. Refrigerate, covered, for 12 hours or longer. Preheat oven to 300 degrees. Bake for 1 hour. Blend remaining soup, brown sugar, cloves and chili powder in small bowl. Spoon over loaves. Bake for 30 minutes longer. Remove loaves to serving platter. Let stand for several minutes for easier slicing. Yield: 10 servings.

Eleanor Rosenquist, Oregon

Easy Sausage Squares

1 pound pork sausage	1/4 teaspoon Tabasco sauce
1/2 cup finely chopped onion	1 cup buttermilk baking mix
1/2 cup shredded Swiss cheese	1/4 cup mayonnaise
1/4 cup Parmesan cheese	3/4 cup milk
2 tablespoons chopped parsley	1 egg yolk, beaten
1 egg, beaten	1 tablespoon water

Preheat oven to 400 degrees. Brown sausage and onion in skillet, stirring until sausage is crumbly; drain well. Add Swiss cheese, Parmesan cheese, parsley, 1 egg and Tabasco sauce; mix well. Combine baking mix, mayonnaise and milk in bowl; mix well. Spoon half the batter into greased 9x9-inch baking pan. Layer sausage mixture and remaining batter on top. Mix 1 egg yolk and water in small bowl. Drizzle over batter and spread with back of spoon. Bake for 20 to 30 minutes or until top is brown. Cool in pan for 5 minutes. Cut into squares. Serve warm or cool. Yield: 9 servings.

Adelaide Marshall, Texas

Sausage Soup

8 ounces hot Italian sausage
2 cups coarsely chopped
  cabbage
1/2 cup chopped green bell
  pepper
2 cloves of garlic, crushed
1/2 teaspoon Italian seasoning

1 can bean and bacon soup
1 1/2 cups water
1/2 cup tomato sauce
1/2 package frozen ravioli,
  cooked
1 (8-ounce) can kidney beans
1/2 cup Parmesan cheese

Slice sausage into 1-inch pieces. Brown sausage evenly in large saucepan; drain. Add cabbage, green pepper, garlic and Italian seasoning. Sauté just until vegetables are tender-crisp. Add soup and water gradually; mix well. Add enough additional water to make of desired consistency. Stir in tomato sauce, ravioli and undrained kidney beans. Simmer until heated through, stirring occasionally. Ladle into soup bowls. Sprinkle with Parmesan cheese. Yield: 6 servings.

Joan Hollingsworth, Maryland

Crock•Pot Cassoulet

1 cup chopped carrots
1/2 cup chopped onion
1/3 cup water
1 (8-ounce) can tomato sauce
1/2 cup dry red wine
1 teaspoon garlic powder
1/2 teaspoon thyme

1/8 teaspoon cloves
2 bay leaves
2 (15-ounce) cans navy beans,
  drained
4 individually frozen chicken
  breast filets
8 ounces Polish sausage, sliced

Bring carrots, onion and water to a boil in saucepan; reduce heat. Simmer, covered, for 5 minutes. Place in 3 1/2 to 4-quart Crock•Pot. Stir in tomato sauce, wine, seasonings and beans. Place frozen chicken and sausage on top of bean mixture. Cook on Low for 9 to 10 hours or on High for 5 1/2 to 6 hours. Remove bay leaves. Yield: 4 servings.

Karen O'Brien, Virginia

♥ *Take soups and stews in the Crock•Pot. Food will stay warm en route and may be kept on Low until serving time after reaching its destination.*

Chicken Pot Roast

1/2 cup all-purpose flour	4 medium potatoes, peeled
Salt and pepper to taste	8 medium carrots
4 chicken breasts	2 medium onions
1/4 cup olive oil	1/2 cup Rosé
2 tablespoons butter or	2 cups water
margarine	2 tablespoons oregano
1 teaspoon minced garlic	1 tablespoon cornstarch

Mix flour, salt and pepper in bowl. Dip chicken in flour mixture, coating well. Heat olive oil and butter in heavy saucepan. Add chicken and garlic. Cook until brown on both sides. Add vegetables, wine and water. Sprinkle with oregano. Simmer for 1 to 1 1/2 hours or until chicken is tender. Remove chicken and vegetables to serving dish. Dissolve cornstarch in a small amount of water. Stir into sauce. Simmer until thickened. Spoon over chicken. Yield: 4 servings.

Jayne Maniche, Ohio

Mexican Chicken Rolls

8 chicken breast filets	1/2 teaspoon salt
4 ounces Monterey Jack cheese	1/4 teaspoon cumin
with jalapeño peppers	1/4 teaspoon pepper
1/2 cup bread crumbs	3/4 cup melted butter or
1/4 cup Parmesan cheese	margarine
1 tablespoon chili powder	

Pound chicken to 1/4-inch thickness. Cut Monterey Jack cheese into 8 strips. Place 1 strip on each piece of chicken. Roll to enclose cheese; tuck ends under. Combine bread crumbs, Parmesan cheese and seasonings in bowl. Dip chicken rolls into butter; coat with seasoned bread crumbs. Place in baking dish. Drizzle with remaining butter. Chill for 4 hours or longer. Preheat oven to 400 degrees. Bake for 25 minutes or until tender. Serve warm or at room temperature with salsa. Yield: 8 servings.

Patio Chicken

1 cup long grain rice
1 (3-pound) chicken, cut up
1 can cream of chicken soup
1 can cream of celery soup
1 envelope dry onion soup mix
1¼ cups white wine

1¼ cups water
½ cup sliced mushrooms
¼ cup chopped green bell
  pepper
¼ cup chopped pimento
Pepper to taste

Preheat oven to 350 degrees. Spread uncooked rice evenly in 4-quart casserole. Arrange chicken pieces over rice. Mix canned soups, dry soup mix, wine and water in bowl. Pour over chicken. Sprinkle mushrooms, green pepper, pimento and pepper over top. Bake, covered, for 1½ hours. Bake, uncovered, for 30 minutes longer or until chicken is golden brown. Yield: 4 servings.

Susan Fitzgerald, Texas

Sonora Chicken Casserole

1½ pounds chicken breast
  filets
1½ cups water
2 tablespoons butter or
  margarine
3 cups chicken-flavored
  stuffing mix

1 teaspoons ground cumin
1 cup mild salsa or picante
  sauce
2 cups shredded Monterey Jack
  cheese with jalapeño peppers
¾ cup sour cream

Preheat oven to 325 degrees. Cook chicken breasts as desired; slice into thin strips. Bring water and butter to a boil in saucepan. Add stuffing mix and cumin; mix well. Spread evenly in 7x12-inch baking dish. Layer chicken, salsa and cheese over stuffing. Bake for 30 minutes. Serve with sour cream. Yield: 6 servings.

Teresa Fletcher, Arizona

Turkey and Noodle Bake

1 cup sliced celery
1/2 cup chopped onion
1 tablespoon butter
9 ounces Velveeta cheese, cubed
1/4 cup milk
2 tablespoons chopped pimento

1 1/2 cups chopped cooked turkey
3 cups cooked noodles
1/2 cup dry bread crumbs
2 tablespoons melted butter
8 strips Cheddar cheese

Preheat oven to 350 degrees. Sauté celery and onion in 1 tablespoon butter in skillet until tender. Add Velveeta cheese and milk. Cook over low heat until cheese melts, stirring constantly. Stir in pimento and turkey. Alternate layers of noodles and turkey mixture in 6x10-inch baking dish. Toss bread crumbs with 2 tablespoons melted butter; sprinkle over casserole. Bake for 25 minutes. Arrange Cheddar cheese strips in lattice over top. Bake until cheese is melted. Yield: 6 servings.

Gail Jones, Illinois

Turkey Divan Rolls

2   (16-ounce) packages individually frozen broccoli spears
1 can cream of chicken soup
1/2 cup mayonnaise
1/2 teaspoon curry powder
1/3 cup cream

2 teaspoons lemon juice
12 very thin slices deli turkey breast
1 cup shredded Cheddar cheese
1 cup stuffing mix
2 tablespoons melted butter or margarine

Preheat oven to 350 degrees. Cook broccoli in a small amount of water until tender; drain. Cover with ice water; drain. Combine soup, mayonnaise, curry powder, cream and lemon juice in bowl; mix well. Spread a small amount in 9x13-inch baking dish. Wrap turkey slices around broccoli spears. Arrange in prepared dish. Spoon remaining sauce over turkey. Sprinkle with cheese and mixture of dry stuffing mix and butter. Bake for 20 minutes or until brown and bubbly. Yield: 6 servings.

Lane Truitt, North Carolina

Crab Casserole

1 cup half and half
1 cup butter or margarine
1 1/2 (5-ounce) jars Old English cheese

2 cups sliced mushrooms
1 pound crab meat
8 ounces fine noodles, cooked
1 cup buttered crumbs

Preheat oven to 350 degrees. Combine half and half, butter and cheese in saucepan. Cook over low heat until cheese and butter melt, stirring constantly. Add mushrooms and crab meat. Layer noodles and crab meat mixture in 2-quart casserole. Sprinkle with crumbs. Bake for 45 minutes or until golden brown and bubbly. Yield: 6 servings.

Mary Johnson, Iowa

Tuna Chowder

8 slices bacon, chopped
2 medium onions, chopped
2 (17-ounce) cans whole kernel
   corn, drained
2 (8-ounce) bottles of clam juice
2 teaspoons sugar
2 teaspoons salt
1/4 teaspoon pepper
6 tablespoons cornstarch
2 quarts half and half
1 teaspoon hot pepper sauce
2 (7-ounce) cans white tuna,
   drained

Sauté bacon in 4-quart saucepan until crisp. Remove bacon from pan. Drain pan, reserving 3 tablespoons bacon drippings. Sauté onions in reserved drippings in saucepan for 2 to 3 minutes or until tender. Stir in corn, clam juice, sugar, salt and pepper. Bring to a simmer over medium heat. Stir in mixture of cornstarch and 1 cup half and half. Stir in remaining half and half gradually. Bring to a boil, stirring constantly. Cook for 1 minute, stirring constantly. Add hot pepper sauce and tuna. Heat to serving temperature, stirring frequently. Stir in bacon. Ladle into serving bowls. Yield: 12 servings.

Faye Cunningham, Washington

Shrimp and Asparagus Casserole

2 cans cream of mushroom soup
2 cups shredded Cheddar
   cheese
1 pound peeled shrimp, cooked
1 (10-ounce) packages frozen
   asparagus, thawed

Preheat oven to 350 degrees. Mix soup and cheese in bowl. Layer shrimp, asparagus and soup mixture 1/2 at a time in 11/2-quart baking dish. Bake for 30 minutes. Yield: 6 servings.

Georgette Morgan, Florida

♥ *Keep a supply of disposable baking dishes in which to deliver casseroles. The gift will be doubly helpful without the inconvenience of returning a dish.*

Seafood Lasagna

10 to 12 lasagna noodles
1 cup chopped onion
2 tablespoons butter or
   margarine
8 ounces cream cheese
1½ cups cottage cheese
1 egg, beaten
2 teaspoons basil
Salt and pepper to taste

⅓ cup milk
2 cans cream of mushroom soup
⅓ cup dry white wine
1 pound cooked shrimp
8 ounces crab meat
¼ cup Parmesan cheese
1 cup shredded Cheddar cheese
8 tomato wedges

Preheat oven to 350 degrees. Cook lasagna noodles using package directions; drain. Rinse with cold water; drain. Sauté onion in butter in saucepan until tender. Cut cream cheese into small pieces. Combine sautéed onion, cream cheese, cottage cheese, egg and seasonings in bowl; mix well. Combine milk, soup and wine in bowl. Reserve several shrimp for garnish. Add remaining shrimp and crab meat to soup mixture; mix well. Alternate layers of noodles, cheese mixture and shrimp mixture ⅓ at a time in greased 9x13-inch baking dish. Sprinkle with Parmesan cheese. Bake for 45 minutes or until bubbly. Top with Cheddar cheese. Bake for 2 minutes longer or until cheese is melted. Let stand for 15 minutes before serving. Garnish with tomato wedges and reserved shrimp. Yield: 12 servings.

Joyce Wexler, Louisiana

Eggs Vermicelli

½ cup chopped green bell
   pepper
½ cup chopped red bell pepper
½ cup butter or margarine
2 tablespoons all-purpose flour

2 cups milk
Salt and pepper to taste
1 teaspoon Tabasco sauce
12 hard-cooked eggs
6 slices crisp-fried bacon

Preheat oven to 350 degrees. Sauté green and red pepper in butter in saucepan. Sprinkle with flour. Add milk gradually. Cook until thickened, stirring constantly. Stir in salt, pepper and Tabasco sauce. Peel eggs; press through sieve into buttered 9x13-inch baking dish. Pour sauce over top. Chill until serving time. Bake for 20 minutes. Top with bacon. Yield: 8 servings.

Linda VanAustin, Florida

♥ *Side Dish Helpers* ♥

Frozen Waldorf Salad

1 (9-ounce) can crushed
   pineapple
2 eggs, slightly beaten
1/2 cup sugar
1/4 cup lemon juice
1/8 teaspoon salt
1/4 cup mayonnaise

1 cup whipped topping
2 1/2 cups chopped unpeeled red
   Delicious apples
2/3 cup chopped celery
1/2 cup chopped walnuts
1/3 cup miniature
   marshmallows

Drain pineapple, reserving syrup. Combine syrup, eggs, sugar, lemon
juice and salt in saucepan. Cook over low heat for 20 minutes or until
slightly thickened, stirring constantly. Cool. Fold in mayonnaise and
whipped topping. Combine pineapple, apples, celery, walnuts and
marshmallows in bowl. Add dressing; mix gently. Spoon into paper-
lined muffin cups. Freeze until firm. Place in refrigerator for 1 hour
before serving. Remove paper liner from each salad; serve on lettuce-
lined serving plates. Yield: 12 servings.

Arlene Bosier, Missouri

Holiday Ambrosia

2 large pineapples
12 large navel oranges
2 cups grated coconut
1/4 cup red maraschino cherries

1/4 cup green maraschino
   cherries
2 cups pineapple yogurt
1 cup grated coconut

Peel and core pineapples. Cut into large chunks. Peel oranges; remove
any seeds. Slice thinly. Layer pineapple, oranges, 2 cups coconut and
cherries in large glass serving bowl. Combine yogurt and 1 cup coconut
in bowl. Spoon into serving dish. Chill yogurt mixture and fruit for 4
hours or longer. Serve ambrosia with yogurt sauce. Yield: 12 servings.

Vesta Arbuckle, Mississippi

Apricot and Pineapple Salad

2 (3-ounce) packages orange
   gelatin
2 cups boiling water
1/2 cup pineapple juice
1/2 cup apricot juice
1 (17-ounce) can crushed
   pineapple, drained
1 (17-ounce) can apricots,
   chopped
2 tablespoons melted butter or
   margarine

3 tablespoons all-purpose flour
1/2 cup sugar
1 egg, slightly beaten
1 cup apricot juice
1 cup pineapple juice
3 ounces cream cheese, softened
1 cup whipped topping
2 cups shredded Cheddar
   cheese

Dissolve gelatin in boiling water in bowl. Add 1/2 cup pineapple juice, 1/2 cup apricot juice, crushed pineapple and apricots; mix well. Pour into 9x13-inch dish. Chill until firm. Blend butter and flour in saucepan. Add sugar, egg, 1 cup apricot juice and 1 cup pineapple juice. Cook until thickened, stirring constantly. Stir in cream cheese. Cool. Fold in whipped topping. Spread over congealed layer. Sprinkle cheese over top. Chill until serving time. Yield: 15 servings.

Dawn Haley, Ohio

Cranberry Salad

1 (3-ounce) package orange
   gelatin
1 (3-ounce) package cherry
   gelatin
1 cup boiling water
1 (16-ounce) can whole
   cranberry sauce

1 cup chopped pecans
1 (6-ounce) can frozen orange
   juice concentrate, thawed
1 (15-ounce) can crushed
   pineapple
1/2 cup coarsely chopped celery

Dissolve gelatins in boiling water in bowl. Add cranberry sauce, pecans, orange juice concentrate, pineapple and celery; mix well. Pour into oiled 6-cup ring mold. Chill until set. Unmold onto serving plate. Yield: 12 servings.

Faye Christiansen, Georgia

♥ *Deliver congealed salads in their molds. They will store better until needed. Include unmolding directions and appropriate garnishes for serving later.*

Strawberry Pretzel Salad

1¹/₂ cups coarsely crushed
  pretzels
4¹/₂ tablespoons sugar
³/₄ cup melted margarine
8 ounces cream cheese, softened
8 ounces whipped topping

³/₄ cup sugar
1 (6-ounce) package strawberry
  gelatin
2 cups boiling water
1 (16-ounce) package frozen
  sliced strawberries

Preheat oven to 350 degrees. Combine pretzels, 4¹/₂ tablespoons sugar and margarine in 9x13-inch baking dish. Spread evenly in dish. Bake for 10 minutes. Cool. Combine cream cheese, whipped topping and ³/₄ cup sugar in bowl; mix well. Spread over crust. Dissolve gelatin in boiling water in bowl. Add strawberries. Chill until partially set. Spoon over cream cheese layer. Chill until set. Yield: 12 servings.

Lovea Vaughan, Florida

Spicy Avocado Salad

3 large ripe avocados
3 large firm tomatoes
2 medium onions

2 tablespoons lemon juice
Freshly ground pepper to taste
Garlic powder to taste

Chop avocados, tomatoes, and onions into bite-sized pieces. Combine in serving bowl. Sprinkle with lemon juice and seasonings; mix gently. Chill in refrigerator until serving time. Yield: 12 servings.

Emily Shear, Illinois

Potato Salad Deluxe

9 medium potatoes, boiled in
  skins
1¹/₂ tablespoons white wine
  vinegar
2 tablespoons sugar
Salt and pepper to taste
¹/₄ cup chopped parsley

6 hard-cooked eggs, peeled,
  chopped
1 (4-ounce) jar chopped
  pimento, drained
¹/₂ cup chopped green onions
3 cups mayonnaise
1 (5-ounce) jar horseradish

Peel and chop cooked potatoes. Combine vinegar, sugar, salt and pepper. Add to warm potatoes. Chill in refrigerator. Add parsley, eggs, pimento and green onions. Chill overnight. Add mayonnaise and horseradish. Chill until serving time. Yield: 8 servings.

Cecile Loudat, Texa

South Seas Salad

1 (6-ounce) package lemon
  gelatin
1/2 teaspoon salt
2 cups boiling water
1 (8-ounce) can crushed
  pineapple
3/4 cup cold water
1/4 white wine vinegar
1/2 cup packed bean sprouts

1/3 cup thinly sliced water
  chestnuts
1 tablespoon sliced pimento
1 tablespoon chopped green
  bell pepper
1/2 cup mayonnaise
1 teaspoon lemon juice
1 tablespoon toasted sesame
  seed

Dissolve gelatin and salt in boiling water in bowl. Stir in undrained pineapple, cold water and wine vinegar. Chill until partially set. Fold in bean sprouts, water chestnuts, pimento and green pepper. Pour into oiled 5½-cup ring mold. Chill until firm. Combine mayonnaise, lemon juice and sesame seed in small bowl; mix well. Unmold salad onto shredded lettuce-lined serving plate. Serve with mayonnaise mixture. Yield: 6 servings.

Betty Morgan, Iowa

Vegetable Salad Special

1 (16-ounce) can cut green beans
1 (16-ounce) can tiny sweet peas
1 (16-ounce) can Shoe Peg corn
1 (2-ounce) jar chopped pimento
1 cup finely chopped celery
1 green bell pepper, chopped
1 small onion, chopped
1/2 cup sugar

1/2 cup wine vinegar
1/2 cup corn oil
2 tablespoons parsley
1 teaspoon salt
1/2 teaspoon dry mustard
1/2 teaspoon tarragon
1/2 teaspoon basil

Drain canned vegetables and pimento. Combine with fresh vegetables in serving bowl. Mix sugar, vinegar, oil and seasonings in small bowl. Pour over vegetables; mix gently. Chill, covered, overnight. Yield: 10 to 12 servings.

June Wheeler, Missouri

Curried Chicken Salad

2 cups mayonnaise
2 tablespoons lemon juice
2¹/2 tablespoons soy sauce
1 tablespoon (rounded) curry
  powder
1 tablespoon onion juice
1 tablespoon chutney, chopped
3 cups chopped cooked chicken
  breasts

1¹/2 cups chopped celery
1 (6-ounce) can sliced water
  chestnuts, drained
2 cups seedless white grapes
1 (16-ounce) can pineapple
  chunks, well drained
¹/2 cup slivered almonds,
  toasted

Combine mayonnaise, lemon juice, soy sauce, curry powder, onion juice and chutney in large bowl; mix well. Add chicken, vegetables and fruit; toss lightly to mix. Refrigerate overnight. Sprinkle with almonds. Yield: 8 servings.

Christine Morrow, Delaware

Layered Chicken Salad

1 small head lettuce, torn
1 (10-ounce) package frozen
  peas, thawed
3 (5-ounce) cans chunky
  chicken
1 cup sour cream
1¹/2 cups mayonnaise
¹/3 cup minced parsley
2¹/2 teaspoons dillweed

1¹/2 teaspoons Beau Monde
  seasoning
¹/4 teaspoon garlic powder
1¹/2 cups shredded carrots
4 hard-cooked eggs, sliced
1¹/2 cups thinly sliced celery
1 small red onion, thinly sliced
¹/4 cup Parmesan cheese
8 slices crisp-fried bacon

Layer lettuce and peas in large salad bowl. Drain chicken, reserving broth. Mix reserved broth, sour cream, mayonnaise, parsley and seasonings in small bowl. Spread half the mixture evenly over peas. Add layers of carrots, chicken, eggs, celery and onion. Spread remaining sour cream mixture over top, sealing to edge of bowl. Sprinkle with Parmesan cheese. Chill, covered, overnight. Sprinkle crumbled bacon on top just before serving. Yield: 12 servings.

Maria Miller, Florida

Ham Salad

1 package wild rice
1 envelope dry vinaigrette
  seasoning mix
1/2 cup sliced green olives
1 cup chopped celery
1 (6-ounce) jar artichoke hearts,
  sliced

1/2 cup chopped cucumber
1/2 cup chopped tomatoes,
  drained
1 cup chopped ham
1/2 to 3/4 cup mayonnaise
Salt and pepper to taste
Onion powder to taste

Cook wild rice using package directions. Prepare vinaigrette mix using package directions. Combine rice and vinaigrette in bowl; mix well. Add olives, celery, artichoke hearts, cucumber, tomatoes, ham, mayonnaise and seasonings; mix well. Chill, covered, overnight. Yield: 12 servings.

Gigi Riggs, Kansas

Ham and Mandarin Salad

1 (7-ounce) package macaroni
  rings, cooked
1 clove of garlic, split
2 cups chopped cooked ham
1/3 cup chopped green onions
1 cup chopped celery

1 (11-ounce) can mandarin
  oranges, drained
2/3 cup mayonnaise
1/4 cup light cream
2 tablespoons vinegar
1/2 teaspoon pepper

Rinse macaroni with cold water; drain. Rub salad bowl with cut side of garlic; discard garlic. Combine macaroni, ham, green onions, celery and orange segments in prepared bowl. Chill, covered, for 2 hours to overnight. Blend mayonnaise, cream, vinegar and pepper in small bowl. Pour over macaroni mixture; toss to coat well. Serve on lettuce-lined plate. Yield: 12 servings.

Louise Baumgartner, Minnesota

♥ *Macaroni and rice salads keep well refrigerated. Deliver them in an airtight refrigerator containers for easy storage along with crisp lettuce leaves for lining serving bowls.*

Shrimp and Rice Salad

1 cup cooked shrimp
3 cups cooked rice
1/4 cup sliced celery
1/4 cup sliced pimento-stuffed
    olives
1/4 cup chopped green bell
    pepper

1/4 cup chopped pimento
1/4 cup minced onion
1/2 teaspoon salt
1/2 teaspoon pepper
3 tablespoons mayonnaise
Tomato wedges
Lemon wedges

Split shrimp lengthwise, reserving several whole shrimp for garnish. Combine with rice, celery, olives, green pepper, pimento and onion in bowl; mix well. Chill, covered, until serving time. Blend salt, pepper and mayonnaise in bowl. Add to shrimp mixture, tossing to mix well. Serve on bed of crisp salad greens. Garnish with tomato wedges, lemon wedges and whole shrimp. Serve with French salad dressing. Yield: 6 servings.

Jeannine Partsch, Nebraska

Creamy Asparagus Casserole

4 (10-ounce) packages frozen
    asparagus spears
1/4 cup butter or margarine
1/4 cup all-purpose flour
1 teaspoon salt
Pepper to taste

Paprika to taste
2 cups milk
6 ounces cream cheese, cubed
1 cup sliced ripe olives
1 cup bread crumbs

Preheat oven to 350 degrees. Cook asparagus using package directions; drain. Melt butter in saucepan. Blend in flour, salt, pepper and paprika. Stir in milk gradually. Cook until smooth and thickened, stirring constantly. Add cream cheese. Heat until cheese is partially melted. Arrange asparagus in 9x13-inch baking dish. Layer olives and 3/4 cup bread crumbs over asparagus. Pour cheese sauce over top. Sprinkle with remaining 1/4 cup bread crumbs. Bake for 20 minutes or until bubbly and golden brown. Yield: 12 servings.

Anita Greer, Delaware

Green Bean Casserole

2 tablespoons butter or
  margarine
1/2 cup cornflake crumbs
1 teaspoon milk recipe ranch
  salad dressing mix
3 tablespoons butter or
  margarine
5 teaspoons milk recipe ranch
  salad dressing mix

3 tablespoons all-purpose flour
1 1/2 cups milk
1/2 cup shredded Cheddar
  cheese
1/2 cup shredded Swiss cheese
2 (10-ounce) packages frozen
  French-style green beans
2 tablespoons slivered
  almonds, toasted

Microwave 2 tablespoons butter in small glass bowl on High until melted. Add cornflake crumbs and 1 teaspoon salad dressing mix; toss to mix. Set aside. Microwave 3 tablespoons butter in medium glass bowl on High until melted. Blend in 5 teaspoons salad dressing mix and flour. Stir in milk gradually. Microwave for 4 minutes or until bubbly and thickened, stirring once. Stir in cheese until melted. Microwave green beans in glass casserole according to package directions. Pour cheese sauce over beans. Microwave for 5 minutes or until bubbly, turning dish once. Sprinkle cornflake mixture and almonds over top. Microwave for 1 minute longer. Let stand for 5 minutes before serving.
Yield: 6 to 8 servings.

Regina Thurgood, Ohio

Broccoli and Wild Rice Casserole

1 (6-ounce) package long grain
  and wild rice mix
20 fresh mushrooms, sliced
1 cup chopped red onion
1 tablespoon butter or
  margarine

1 bunch fresh broccoli
1 pound Monterey Jack cheese,
  shredded
Paprika to taste

Preheat oven to 375 degrees. Cook wild rice mix according to package directions. Sauté mushrooms and onion in butter in saucepan. Add rice; mix well. Spread in 9x13-inch baking dish. Trim broccoli; cut into spears. Cook in a small amount of water in saucepan until tender-crisp; drain. Arrange over rice. Top with cheese and paprika. Bake for 15 minutes or until bubbly. Yield: 8 servings.

Tammy Yates, Colorado

Corn Casserole

1 egg, beaten
1 cup sour cream
1/2 cup melted margarine
1 (8-ounce) can cream-style corn

1 (8-ounce) can whole kernel corn
1 (8-ounce) package corn muffin mix

Preheat oven to 350 degrees. Combine all ingredients in order listed in bowl; mix well. Pour into greased 9x9-inch baking dish. Bake for 40 to 55 minutes or until toothpick inserted in center comes out clean. Serve hot. Yield: 8 servings.

Mary Ann Eisenmann, Iowa

Easy Potato Casserole

2 (16-ounce) packages frozen hashed brown potatoes
1 (13-ounce) can evaporated milk

2 cans Cheddar cheese soup
Salt and pepper to taste
1 (8-ounce) can French-fried onion rings

Preheat oven to 350 degrees. Combine potatoes, evaporated milk, soup, seasonings and half the onion rings in greased 9x13-inch baking dish. Bake for 45 minutes or until potatoes are tender. Sprinkle with remaining onion rings. Yield: 6 to 8 servings.

Patricia Moore, Missouri

Cheesy Spinach

1 tablespoon corn oil
1/4 cup dry bread crumbs
3 eggs
1 (10-ounce) package frozen chopped spinach, thawed
1/2 cup Romano cheese

1 (16-ounce) container ricotta cheese
2 cups shredded mozzarella cheese
Salt and pepper to taste

Preheat oven to 350 degrees. Coat bottom and side of 8-inch baking dish with oil. Sprinkle with bread crumbs, coating evenly. Beat eggs in mixer bowl. Drain spinach well. Add spinach and cheese to eggs; mix well. Season with salt and pepper. Pour into prepared dish. Bake for 45 minutes or until browned. Yield: 6 servings.

Lillian Diefendorff, Kentucky

Mixed Vegetable Bake

1 can cream of mushroom soup
2/3 cup milk
8 ounces cream cheese
2 cups shredded Cheddar
  cheese

2 (1-pound) packages frozen
   mixed vegetables
3 cups herb-seasoned stuffing
   mix

Preheat oven to 300 degrees. Combine soup, milk, cream cheese and 1½ cups Cheddar cheese in saucepan. Cook over medium heat until cheese is melted, stirring constantly. Cook vegetables according to package directions; drain well. Mix sauce and vegetables in 9x13-inch baking dish. Mix stuffing mix with remaining ½ cup Cheddar cheese. Sprinkle over vegetable mixture. Bake for 30 minutes or until brown and bubbly. Yield: 12 servings.

Ann Tomlinson, Indiana

Vegetable Medley Casserole

1 (8-ounce) package frozen
   cauliflower
1 (10-ounce) package frozen
   broccoli cuts
1 (16-ounce) package frozen
   whole kernel corn
1 (17-ounce) can cream-style
   corn

1 (3-ounce) can mushrooms,
   drained
2 cups shredded Cheddar
   cheese
1 can celery soup
1½ cups bread crumbs
2 tablespoons melted butter or
   margarine

Preheat oven to 375 degrees. Cook cauliflower, broccoli and whole kernel corn according to package directions; drain well. Combine with cream-style corn, mushrooms, cheese and soup in bowl; mix well. Spoon into 9x13-baking dish. Toss bread crumbs with butter in small bowl. Sprinkle over casserole. Bake for 30 minutes. Let stand for 10 minutes before serving. Yield: 10 servings.

Melanie Platt, Michigan

♥ *Dessert Helpers* ♥

Wonderful Baked Apples

1/2 pound cake
8 Granny Smith apples, peeled, cored
1/4 cup melted butter or margarine
1/2 (10-ounce) jar nesselrode or mincemeat

1/4 cup packed light brown sugar
2 tablespoons seedless raisins
Grated rind and juice of 1 lemon
2 tablespoons butter or margarine

Preheat oven to 275 degrees. Crumble cake onto baking sheet. Bake until crumbs are dry. Increase oven temperature to 375 degrees. Coat apples with 1/4 cup melted butter. Roll in crumbs, coating well. Place in 9x13-inch baking dish. Combine nesselrode, brown sugar, raisins, lemon rind and lemon juice in small bowl; mix well. Spoon into centers of apples. Dot with 2 tablespoons butter. Pour a small amount of hot water around apples in dish. Bake for 45 to 55 minutes or until apples are tender. Spoon pan juices over hot apples. Cool. Serve at room temperature. Omit 2 tablespoons raisins when using mincemeat. Yield: 8 servings.

Nelda Banks, Kentucky

Cool Banana Pudding

2 (3-ounce) packages banana instant pudding mix
3 cups cold milk
1 (14-ounce) can sweetened condensed milk

1 (12-ounce) container whipped topping
1 (15-ounce) package vanilla wafers
4 or 5 medium bananas, sliced

Prepare pudding mix according to package directions using 3 cups milk. Fold in sweetened condensed milk and 1 cup whipped topping. Layer vanilla wafers, bananas and pudding mixture 1/2 at a time in 9x13-inch dish. Top with remaining whipped topping. Chill, covered with plastic wrap, until serving time. Yield: 16 servings.

Marie E. Rice, Alabama

Ruby Oranges

1 cup sugar	1/4 teaspoon ginger
1 1/3 cups cranberry juice	2 strips orange rind
4 whole cloves	2 strips lemon rind
1 cinnamon stick	8 navel oranges

Dissolve sugar in 2/3 cup cranberry juice in saucepan. Simmer over low heat for 10 minutes. Add cranberry juice, cloves, cinnamon stick, ginger and orange and lemon rind. Cook until liquid is reduced to a thick syrup. Strain. Peel and slice oranges very thinly. Place oranges in serving dish. Pour syrup over oranges. Chill for several hours. Yield: 6 to 8 servings.

Donna McDonald, Indiana

Spicy Microwaved Fruit

2 (16-ounce) cans pear halves, drained	1/2 teaspoon cinnamon
	1/8 teaspoon cloves
4 medium apples, peeled, sliced	1/8 teaspoon allspice
2 cups whole cranberry sauce	1/2 cup pear syrup

Cut pears into halves lengthwise. Layer pears and apples in 1 1/2-quart glass baking dish. Combine cranberry sauce, spices and pear syrup in bowl; mix well. Spoon over fruit. Microwave, covered, on High for 2 to 3 minutes; stir. Microwave for 3 to 4 minutes longer. Yield: 6 to 8 servings.

Paula Pelham, Texas

Chocolate Éclair Dessert

1 (16-ounce) package graham crackers	2 squares baking chocolate
	1 teaspoon vanilla extract
2 (3-ounce) packages vanilla instant pudding mix	1 1/2 cups confectioners' sugar
	3 tablespoons light corn syrup
3 1/2 cups milk	3 tablespoons melted butter
9 ounces whipped topping	3 tablespoons milk

Line 9x13-inch dish with graham crackers. Prepare pudding mix according to package directions using 3 1/2 cups milk. Fold in topping. Spread half the pudding mixture over crackers. Repeat layers, ending with crackers. Melt chocolate in saucepan over low heat. Add vanilla, confectioners' sugar, corn syrup, butter and 3 tablespoons milk. Spread over graham crackers. Chill overnight. Yield: 15 to 18 servings.

LaDonna M. Smith, Texas

Chocolate Refrigerator Dessert

2 cups semisweet chocolate
  chips
2 cups milk
2 tablespoons unflavored
  gelatin
1/4 cup cold water

1/4 cup sugar
2 teaspoons vanilla extract
1 cup whipping cream, whipped
20 unfilled ladyfingers, split
2 cups whipping cream
1 tablespoon sugar

Combine chocolate chips and milk in double boiler. Heat until chocolate is melted, stirring occasionally. Soften gelatin in cold water for 5 minutes. Add softened gelatin and 1/4 cup sugar to chocolate mixture. Cook until gelatin dissolves, stirring constantly. Remove from heat. Beat with rotary beater until smooth. Add vanilla. Chill mixture until thickened. Fold whipped cream into chocolate mixture. Line bottom and side of springform pan with ladyfingers. Pour half the chocolate mixture over ladyfingers. Arrange remaining ladyfingers on top. Pour remaining chocolate over ladyfingers. Refrigerate until serving time. Remove side of pan. Whip 2 cups whipping cream with 1 tablespoon sugar in bowl until soft peaks form. Serve with cake. Yield: 8 to 10 servings.

Jeanne Clark, North Carolina

Super Pineapple Split

1/4 cup butter or margarine,
  softened
2 cups confectioners' sugar
1/2 cup semisweet chocolate
  chips
1 1/2 cups evaporated milk
1 (12-ounce) package vanilla
  wafers, crushed
1/2 cup butter, softened
8 ounces cream cheese, softened

1/4 cup butter, softened
1 (20-ounce) can crushed
  pineapple, drained
2 large bananas
2 tablespoons lemon juice
1/2 cup coarsely chopped pecans
1 (16-ounce) container whipped
  topping
1 (3-ounce) jar maraschino
  cherries, drained

Combine first 4 ingredients in saucepan. Cook until thick and smooth, stirring constantly. Cool. Mix vanilla wafer crumbs and 1/2 cup butter in bowl. Press over bottom of 9x13-inch baking dish. Beat cream cheese and 1/4 cup butter in bowl until well blended. Add 2/3 cup pineapple; mix well. Spread over crust. Slice bananas 1/2 inch thick. Drizzle with lemon juice; drain well. Arrange over cream cheese layer. Top with chocolate sauce. Sprinkle pecans over sauce. Spread whipped topping over all. Sprinkle with remaining pineapple and cherries. Chill for several hours. Yield: 12 servings.

Jane Moonen, Georgia

Frosty Pumpkin Squares

1 cup melted butter or
  margarine
2 cups all-purpose flour
1/2 cup packed light brown
  sugar
1 cup chopped pecans
3 (3-ounce) packages peach
  gelatin

1 cup boiling water
1 (30-ounce) can pumpkin pie
  filling
1 tablespoon pumpkin pie spice
1 teaspoon nutmeg
1 quart vanilla ice cream,
  chopped

Preheat oven to 350 degrees. Combine butter, flour, brown sugar and pecans in 9x13-inch glass baking dish. Bake for 12 to 15 minutes or microwave on High for 5 minutes, stirring several times. Reserve 1 cup mixture. Press remaining mixture over bottom of dish with fork. Dissolve gelatin in boiling water. Add pumpkin pie filling and spices. Bring to boil, stirring constantly. Remove from heat. Add ice cream; stir until smooth. Pour over crust. Sprinkle with reserved crumbs. Chill until firm. Cut into squares. Serve with whipped cream. Yield: 15 servings.

Emily Griffen, Missouri

Lemon Whip

3/4 cup butter or margarine,
  softened
2/3 cup ground walnuts
1 1/2 cups all-purpose flour
8 ounces cream cheese, softened
1/2 cup confectioners' sugar

1 cup whipped topping
2 (4-ounce) packages lemon
  instant pudding mix
3 cups milk
1 tablespoon lemon juice
1 cup whipped topping

Preheat oven to 350 degrees. Combine butter, walnuts and flour in bowl; mix until crumbly. Press into 9x13-inch baking pan. Bake for 20 minutes. Cool. Beat cream cheese and confectioners' sugar until fluffy. Fold in 1 cup whipped topping. Spread over crust. Beat pudding mix, milk and lemon juice in bowl for 1 minute. Pour over cream cheese layer. Chill for 10 minutes. Top with 1 cup whipped topping. Chill for 3 to 4 hours. Garnish with additional walnuts. Yield: 12 to 16 servings.

Marjorie Parks, Arizona

Winter Fruit Compote

1 (28-ounce) can peach halves
1 (28-ounce) can pear halves
1 (16-ounce) can apricot halves
1 cup packed light brown sugar
2 tablespoons all-purpose flour
1 teaspoon vanilla extract

12 ounces cream cheese,
   softened
5 teaspoons honey
1 (8-ounce) jar maraschino
   cherries

Preheat oven to 375 degrees. Drain peaches, pears and apricots, reserving 1¼ cups mixed juices. Arrange fruit cut sides up in 9x13-inch baking dish. Combine brown sugar, flour, vanilla and 1 cup reserved juices in saucepan. Cook until thickened, stirring constantly. Pour around fruit. Combine cream cheese and honey in mixer bowl. Beat until well blended. Add enough remaining ¼ cup juices to make of the desired consistency, beating until fluffy. Place 1 spoonful of the cream cheese mixture on each piece fruit. Top each with cherry. Bake for 20 minutes or until heated through. Yield: 12 servings.

Marian Butler, West Virginia

Strawberry Butter Torte

¼ cup melted butter or
   margarine
1 cup vanilla wafer crumbs
½ cup butter or margarine,
   softened
2½ cups confectioners' sugar

2 eggs
1½ cups sliced fresh
   strawberries
1 cup whipping cream
¼ cup sugar
½ cup vanilla wafer crumbs

Combine ¼ cup melted butter and 1 cup crumbs in bowl; mix well. Press over bottom of 8x8-inch dish. Combine remaining ½ cup softened butter and confectioners' sugar in mixer bowl. Beat until light and fluffy. Add eggs; beat well. Spread over crumbs. Spoon strawberries on top. Whip cream with sugar in bowl until soft peaks form. Spread over strawberries. Sprinkle remaining ½ cup crumbs on top. Store in refrigerator. Yield: 8 to 10 servings.

Carol Deeds, Kansas

Frozen Strawberry Delight

1 cup all-purpose flour
1/2 cup chopped pecans
1/4 cup packed light brown
  sugar
1/2 cup melted butter or
  margarine
1 (10-ounce) package frozen
  strawberries

3 egg whites
1 cup sugar
1 tablespoon lemon juice
1 teaspoon salt
1 teaspoon vanilla extract
1 (16-ounce) container whipped
  topping

Preheat oven to 350 degrees. Combine first 4 ingredients in bowl; mix well. Spread on baking sheet. Bake for 15 minutes, stirring frequently. Cool. Crumble into 9x13-inch pan, reserving a small amount for topping. Combine thawed strawberries, egg whites, sugar, lemon juice and salt in large mixer bowl. Beat until stiff peaks form. Fold in vanilla and whipped topping. Spoon into prepared pan. Top with reserved crumbs. Freeze overnight. Yield: 12 to 15 servings.

Kathy Dorson, Missouri

Sunny Croissant Pudding

3 tablespoons raisins
1/3 cup warm water
1 cup plus 3 tablespoons
  whipping cream
1 cup plus 2 tablespoons milk
1 vanilla bean, split lengthwise
Pinch of salt
4 eggs

3/4 cup sugar
4 small croissants, cut into
  1/2-inch slices
3 tablespoons melted butter or
  margarine
3 tablespoons confectioners'
  sugar

Preheat oven to 375 degrees. Plump raisins in water in bowl for 30 minutes. Bring cream, milk, vanilla bean and salt to a simmer in double boiler. Beat eggs and sugar in medium bowl. Whisk in cream mixture very gradually. Remove vanilla bean; scrape seed from bean into cream mixture; mix well. Brush croissant slices lightly with melted butter. Arrange in 1-quart soufflé dish. Sprinkle with raisins. Strain custard over croissant slices; press slices gently to absorb liquid. Sprinkle with 1 tablespoon confectioners' sugar. Place in large baking pan. Add 1 inch hot water to large pan. Bake for 45 to 50 minutes or until tester inserted in center comes out clean. Spoon pudding onto plates. Sprinkle with remaining 2 tablespoons confectioners' sugar. Serve hot. Yield: 6 servings.

Melissa Sanders, Ohio

Milky Way Cake

6 Milky Way candy bars
1/2 cup butter or margarine
2 cups sugar
1/2 cup butter or margarine,
   softened
4 eggs
21/2 cups sifted all-purpose flour

1/2 teaspoon soda
13/4 cups buttermilk
1 teaspoon vanilla extract
1 cup chopped pecans
6 ounces milk chocolate chips
2 tablespoons butter or
   margarine

Preheat oven to 350 degrees. Melt candy bars and 1/2 cup butter in saucepan over low heat, stirring to mix well. Set aside. Cream sugar and 1/2 cup butter in mixer bowl until light and fluffy. Beat in eggs 1 at a time. Add mixture of flour and soda alternately with buttermilk, beginning and ending with flour and mixing well after each addition. Stir in melted Milky Way bars, vanilla and pecans. Pour into greased and floured 10-inch tube pan. Bake for 1 hour and 10 minutes or until cake tests done. Cool in pan. Invert onto serving plate. Melt chocolate chips with 2 tablespoons butter in double boiler over hot water. Drizzle slowly over cake. Yield: 16 servings.

Cheryl Davis, New York

Gingery Spice Loaves

1 (14-ounce) package
   gingerbread mix
1 (18-ounce) package lemon
   cake mix
1 cup water

6 eggs
1 cup water
11/2 cups raisins
11/2 cups chopped nuts

Preheat oven to 375 degrees. Combine gingerbread mix, cake mix and 1 cup water in mixer bowl. Beat at medium speed for 2 minutes or until smooth. Add eggs and 1 cup water. Beat at low speed for 1 minute. Beat at medium speed for 1 minute. Fold in raisins and nuts. Pour into 2 greased and floured 5x9-inch loaf pans. Bake for 20 to 25 minutes or until loaves test done. Cool in pan for 10 minutes. Remove to wire rack to cool completely. Yield: 2 loaves.

Karen Shubert, California

Refrigerator Gingerbread Muffins

1/2 cup raisins
1/2 cup chopped pecans
4 cups all-purpose flour
1/8 teaspoon salt
2 teaspoons ginger
1/2 teaspoon cinnamon
1/4 teaspoon allspice

2 teaspoons soda
1 cup buttermilk
1 cup butter or margarine,
    softened
1 cup sugar
4 eggs
1 cup molasses

Toss raisins and pecans with a small amount of flour in bowl, coating well. Sift remaining flour with salt and spices into bowl. Stir soda into buttermilk. Cream butter and sugar in mixer bowl until light and fluffy. Blend in eggs and molasses. Add flour mixture alternately with buttermilk, mixing well after each addition. Stir in raisins and pecans. Store in airtight container in refrigerator for up to 1 month. Place in gift container and include instructions for baking mix in greased muffin cups at 400 degrees for 15 to 18 minutes or until muffins test done. Yield: 4 dozen.

Vicky Stevens, Kansas

Lemon Angel Roll

1 package (1-step) angel food
    cake mix
1 (21-ounce) can lemon pie
    filling
1/2 cup confectioners' sugar
8 ounces cream cheese, softened

1/2 cup butter or margarine,
    softened
4 cups confectioners' sugar
1 teaspoon vanilla extract
1 cup confectioners' sugar
1 to 2 tablespoons lemon juice

Preheat oven to 350 degrees. Combine cake mix and pie filling in mixer bowl. Beat until well blended. Spread in ungreased 10x15-inch cake pan. Bake for 20 to 25 minutes or until cake tests done. Invert onto towel sprinkled with 1/2 cup confectioners' sugar. Roll up cake in towel. Cool. Beat cream cheese and butter in mixer bowl until light and fluffy. Add 4 cups confectioners' sugar and vanilla; beat until smooth. Unroll cake. Spread with cream cheese mixture. Roll as for jelly roll. Place on serving plate. Mix 1 cup confectioners' sugar with enough lemon juice to make of glaze consistency. Drizzle over cake roll. Yield: 16 servings.

Debra Middleton, Texas

Banana Cream Pie

3 cups milk
4 1/2 tablespoons (heaping)
   all-purpose flour
1 1/2 tablespoons (heaping)
   cornstarch
3/4 cup sugar
1/4 teaspoon salt

2 eggs, slightly beaten
1 teaspoon vanilla extract
2 to 4 bananas, sliced
1 baked 9-inch pie shell
1 (8-ounce) container whipped
   topping

Scald milk in double boiler. Combine flour, cornstarch, sugar and salt; mix well. Add to scalded milk. Cook for 15 minutes, stirring constantly. Stir a small amount of hot mixture into beaten eggs; stir eggs into hot mixture. Cook for several minutes longer. Cool. Stir in vanilla. Layer pudding and bananas 1/2 at a time in pie shell. Spread whipped topping over pie. Chill in refrigerator. Yield: 6 to 8 servings.

Shirley Maher, Missouri

Fruit Tart

1 package refrigerator sugar
   cookie dough
8 ounces cream cheese, softened
1/3 cup sugar
1/2 teaspoon vanilla extract
2 cups strawberry halves
2 kiwifruit, peeled, thinly sliced

1 1/2 cups grape halves
1 (8-ounce) can mandarin
   oranges, drained
1 to 2 tablespoons orange
   marmalade
1 tablespoon water

Preheat oven to 375 degrees. Spray round 14-inch pan with nonstick cooking spray. Slice cookie dough 1/8-inch thick. Arrange overlapping slices to form scalloped edge around rim of pan. Arrange remaining slices over bottom of pan, overlapping edges. Bake for 10 minutes or until light brown. Cool completely. Combine cream cheese, sugar and vanilla in bowl. Beat until light. Spread over crust. Arrange fruit in decreasing circles over creamed layer, beginning with strawberries around outside rim. Chill until serving time. Heat marmalade and water in saucepan until well mixed, stirring constantly. Brush over fruit. Cut into wedges to serve. Yield: 12 servings.

Lois Isaacs, Vermont

Frozen Lime Pie

10 tablespoons butter or
  margarine
1 (5-ounce) package salted
  pretzels, finely crushed
1/2 cup sugar
31/2 tablespoons lime juice

1 (14-ounce) can sweetened
  condensed milk
1 drop of green food coloring
21/2 cups whipping cream,
  whipped

Microwave butter in greased 9-inch pie plate on High for 30 seconds or until melted. Stir in pretzels and sugar. Press firmly over bottom and side of pie plate, forming rim above edge. Freeze until firm. Combine lime juice, condensed milk and food coloring in small bowl; mix well. Fold gently into whipped cream. Pour into prepared crust. Freeze for 8 hours or longer. Let stand at room temperature for 15 minutes before serving. Garnish with pretzels. Yield: 10 servings.

Bev McConaughey, Kansas

Pecan and Chocolate Pie

1 stick pie crust mix
2 tablespoons chopped pecans
3 eggs, beaten
1 cup sugar
2 tablespoons melted butter or
  margarine
1/2 cup whipping cream

1/2 cup dark corn syrup
1/2 teaspoon salt
1/4 cup Brandy
1 cup pecan halves
1/2 cup semisweet chocolate
  chips
1 teaspoon vanilla extract

Preheat oven to 375 degrees. Crumble pie crust mix into bowl. Add chopped pecans. Prepare pastry according to package directions. Fit into 9-inch pie plate. Combine eggs, sugar, butter, whipping cream, corn syrup and salt in bowl; mix well. Stir in Brandy, pecan halves, chocolate chips and vanilla. Pour into prepared pie plate. Bake for 40 to 50 minutes or until filling is set. Cool on wire rack. Yield: 8 servings.

Ginger Logan, Nevada

Brownie Pies

2 cups chocolate chips
1 cup butter or margarine
3/4 cup all-purpose flour
2 cups sugar
4 eggs

1/2 teaspoon vanilla extract
1/2 cup milk
2 cups chopped nuts
2 unbaked 9-inch deep-dish pie
   shells

Preheat oven to 350 degrees. Melt chocolate chips and butter in saucepan over low heat. Combine flour and sugar in bowl. Beat eggs, vanilla and milk in bowl. Add flour mixture and chocolate mixture; mix well. Add nuts; mix well. Pour into pie shells. Bake for 45 minutes. Serve warm with vanilla ice cream. Yield: 2 pies.

Nancy Carol Mann, West Virginia

Strawberry Glacé Pie

1/2 cup butter or margarine,
   softened
3 tablespoons sugar
1 egg yolk
1 cup all-purpose flour
1 cup flaked coconut
1/2 cup sugar

1 teaspoon lemon juice
8 ounces cream cheese, softened
1 quart strawberries
1 cup sugar
3 tablespoons cornstarch
1 cup whipped cream

Preheat oven to 325 degrees. Cream butter and 3 tablespoons sugar in mixer bowl until light and fluffy. Blend in egg yolk. Stir in flour and coconut. Press over bottom and side of 9-inch pie plate; flute edge. Prick with fork. Bake for 25 minutes or until light brown. Cool on wire rack. Cream 1/2 cup sugar, lemon juice and cream cheese in bowl until light and fluffy. Spread in cooled pie shell. Arrange enough whole strawberries stem end down in pie shell to cover filling. Chill in refrigerator. Mash and strain remaining strawberries to extract juice. Add enough water to strawberry juice to measure 1 1/2 cups. Bring strawberry juice to a boil in saucepan. Add mixture of 1 cup sugar and cornstarch gradually, stirring constantly. Cook for 1 minute, stirring constantly. Cool. Spoon glaze over strawberries. Chill for several hours. Top with whipped cream.
Yield: 6 servings.

Mary Kearns, Nebraska

Equivalent Chart

	When the recipe calls for	Use
Baking	½ cup butter	¼ pound
	2 cups butter	1 pound
	4 cups all-purpose flour	1 pound
	4½ to 5 cups sifted cake flour	1 pound
	1 square chocolate	1 ounce
	1 cup semisweet chocolate pieces	6 ounces
	4 cups marshmallows	1 pound
	2¼ cups packed brown sugar	1 pound
	4 cups confectioners' sugar	1 pound
	2 cups granulated sugar	1 pound
Cereal – Bread	1 cup fine dry bread crumbs	4 to 5 slices
	1 cup soft bread crumbs	2 slices
	1 cup small bread cubes	2 slices
	1 cup fine cracker crumbs	28 saltines
	1 cup fine graham cracker crumbs	15 crackers
	1 cup vanilla wafer crumbs	22 wafers
	1 cup crushed cornflakes	3 cups uncrushed
	4 cups cooked macaroni	8 ounces
	3½ cups cooked rice	1 cup uncooked
Dairy	1 cup shredded cheese	4 ounces
	1 cup cottage cheese	8 ounces
	1 cup sour cream	8 ounces
	1 cup whipped cream	½ cup heavy cream
	⅔ cup evaporated milk	1 small can
	1⅔ cups evaporated milk	1 13-ounce can
Fruit	4 cups sliced or chopped apples	4 medium
	1 cup mashed banana	3 medium
	2 cups pitted cherries	4 cups unpitted
	3 cups shredded coconut	½ pound
	4 cups cranberries	1 pound
	1 cup pitted dates	1 8-ounce package
	1 cup candied fruit	1 8-ounce package
	3 to 4 tablespoons lemon juice plus 1 tablespoon grated lemon rind	1 lemon
	⅓ cup orange juice plus 2 teaspoons grated orange rind	1 orange
	4 cups sliced peaches	8 medium
	2 cups pitted prunes	1 12-ounce package
	3 cups raisins	1 15-ounce package

	When the recipe calls for	Use
Meat	4 cups chopped cooked chicken 3 cups chopped cooked meat 2 cups cooked ground meat	1 5-pound chicken 1 pound, cooked 1 pound, cooked
Nuts	1 cup chopped nuts	4 ounces shelled 1 pound unshelled
Vegetables	2 cups cooked green beans 2½ cups lima beans or red beans 4 cups shredded cabbage 1 cup grated carrots 1 4-ounce can mushrooms 1 cup chopped onion 4 cups sliced or chopped potatoes 2 cups canned tomatoes	½ pound fresh or 1 16-ounce can 1 cup dried, cooked 1 pound 1 large ½ pound fresh 1 large 4 medium 1 16-ounce can

Measurement Equivalents

1 tablespoon = 3 teaspoons 2 tablespoons = 1 ounce 4 tablespoons = ¼ cup 5⅓ tablespoons = ⅓ cup 8 tablespoons = ½ cup 12 tablespoons = ¾ cup 16 tablespoons = 1 cup 1 cup = 8 ounces or ½ pint 4 cups = 1 quart 4 quarts = 1 gallon	1 6½ to 8-ounce can = 1 cup 1 10½ to 12-ounce can = 1¼ cups 1 14 to 16-ounce can = 1¾ cups 1 16 to 17-ounce can = 2 cups 1 18 to 20-ounce can = 2½ cups 1 20-ounce can = 3½ cups 1 46 to 51-ounce can = 5¾ cups 1 6½- pound to 7½- pound can (No. 10) = 12 or 13 cups

Metric Equivalents

Liquid	Dry
1 teaspoon = 5 milliliters 1 tablespoon = 15 milliliters 1 fluid ounce = 30 milliliters 1 cup = 250 milliliters 1 pint = 500 milliliters	1 quart = 1 liter 1 ounce = 30 grams 1 pound = 450 grams 2.2 pounds = 1 kilogram

NOTE: *The metric measures are approximate benchmarks for purposes of home food preparation.*

Index

FOR ORDERING INFORMATION

Favorite Recipes Press
a division of Great American Opportunities, Inc.
P.O. Box 305142, Nashville, TN 37230
or
Call Toll-free
1-800-251-1542